Design by Contract, by Exam

D1239813

RATE DUE

Richard Mitchell
Jim McKim

ADDISON-WESLEY

Boston • San Francisco • New York • Toronto • Montreal
London • Munich • Paris • Madrid
Capetown • Sydney • Tokyo • Singapore • Mexico City

Pearson Education Corporate Sales Division
201 W. 103rd Street
Indianapolis, IN 46290
(800) 428-5331
corpsales@pearsoned.com

Visit AW on the Web: www.awl.com/cseng/

Library of Congress Cataloging-in-Publication Data

Mitchell, Richard, 1947-
　　Design by contract, by example / Richard Mitchell, Jim McKim.
　　　　p.　cm.
　　Includes bibliographical references and index.
　　ISBN 0-201-63460-0 (pbk.)
　　1. Object-oriented programming (Computer science).　2. Computer-aided design.
　I. McKim, Jim.　II. Title.

　QA76.64 .M592 2002
　005.1'17—dc21

　　　　　　　　　　　　　　　　　　　　　　2001046451

11-12-02

ISBN 0-201-63460-0
Text printed on recycled paper
1 2 3 4 5 6 7 8 9 10—MA—0504030201
First printing, October 2001

Contents

Foreword

The concept of Design by Contract was invented to provide practicing software developers with a way to produce, at little extra cost, software that is much more reliable than is the norm today. Based on a simple metaphor, Design by Contract has applications throughout the process of building software, from analysis and design to implementation, documentation, debugging, even project management.

The ideas are rooted in work on formal—meaning mathematical—approaches to software construction, but do not require the potentially intimidating effort of full formality. In fact, they are incredibly easy to apply; as James McKim likes to say, "if you can write a program, you can write a contract." Yet the benefits are almost immediate, especially if you can find direct support in the programming language and environment, as is the case with Eiffel, which the authors use to introduce the concepts, complemented by applications to Java and other languages.

Mitchell and McKim have produced a clear, concise, and convincing presentation of Design by Contract, filled with examples and patterns, and covering analysis as well as implementation. It derives from years of teaching these concepts to successive generations of both students and professionals, and applying them to constantly new problems.

It's hard to think of many other books that—besides being pleasurable to read—will at so little effort, regardless of your education, experience, programming style and application domain, almost certainly make you, instantly, a better programmer.

—Bertrand Meyer

Preface

WHAT THE BOOK COVERS

Design by contract is all about adding assertions to object-oriented programs, at the design and coding stages. Assertions are facts about a program that must be true for the program to be bug-free. The key assertions in design by contract define preconditions, postconditions, and invariants:

- A precondition is a condition on a method specifying what must be true for it to be valid to call the method.
- A postcondition is a condition on a method specifying what will become true when the method successfully completes.
- An invariant is a condition on a whole class specifying what is true about any object of the class whenever you can call a method on that object.

The assertions are written in a programming language, so that

- They make sense to programmers, providing good, helpful documentation.
- They can be checked at runtime, providing support for testing and debugging.

This book concentrates on showing you how to write good contracts. The book presents six principles for writing good contracts, and some supporting guidelines. Through examples, the book motivates the principles and guidelines and shows them in use.

After studying the first three chapters, you will be in a position to write high-quality contracts. The rest of the book will help you do even better.

In addition to chapters that develop contracts for individual example classes, there are chapters on contracts in relation to inheritance and on the topic of frame rules (contracts that assert what does *not* change). Two larger examples towards the end of the book involve developing contracts across more than one class. Chapter 9 concerns the Observer pattern from Gamma et al. [1994], and Chapter 10 presents a small application in which an object in the user interface is shown to respect part of a contract in the heart of the application. Chapter 12 discusses the use of contracts in systems analysis. Chapter 8 reviews the benefits of using contracts and compares design by contract to defensive programming. Chapter 11 explores how to attach contracts to interfaces and explores briefly how you might implement contracts in a distributed environment.

PROGRAMMING LANGUAGES

The examples are presented first in the object-oriented programming language Eiffel. We chose Eiffel for three reasons:

1. Eiffel has built-in support for contracts, so it is excellent for showing the concepts at work.
2. Eiffel is easy to read, so it's a good pseudo-code from which you can implement the ideas in any object-oriented programming language.
3. Commercial-strength compilers are available for Eiffel, so our contracts can play both their intended roles, as specifications and as checks. A contract is a *specification* of a class, describing precisely what services the class delivers. The assertions in a contract can be evaluated at runtime to *check* that the implementing code is consistent with its specification.

You don't have to be an Eiffel programmer to follow the examples. We are sure you'll be able to carry the principles over to your own programming environment. The issues we raise, and the advice we give, are not specific to Eiffel.

We do rework two of our examples in Java, using a preprocessor (called iContract) that provides support for contracts. This allows us to explore some issues that do not arise so directly in Eiffel and to show you contracts in another language.

WHO THE BOOK IS FOR

The book is written for anyone who wants to find out how to write good contracts. We intend it to be useful to practitioners, students (especially the early chapters), teachers, and researchers.

We don't believe the book is one you can curl up with by the fire (in winter) or the pool (in summer) and read your way through. We believe its material has to be studied and, most importantly, tried out. We hope you have access to a programming environment that supports contracts, such as a Java compiler and the iContract tool (see the bibliography for more information) or an Eiffel compiler (again, more information in the bibliography).

We do not teach object-oriented programming. We assume you know how to program in some object-oriented programming language. We have tried to give enough explanation of the Eiffel and Java code that those familiar with other OO languages can follow the examples.

STYLE

The book is based firmly on examples. Usually, a chapter is based on a single example. This means that there is quite a lot of code to wade through at times. However, most of the code is at the level of assertions, which define what a piece of program achieves. This level of code is generally easier to understand than the code that defines how a piece of program achieves its goal. In addition, we usually dissect the code a few lines at a time to make it easier to follow the discussion.

The examples are mostly simple ones. For example, instead of writing full contracts for the customer manager component introduced in Chapter 1, we write them for a look-up table (or dictionary), which is the data structure that underpins the customer manager component. That way, you won't get lost in too many details, and you won't lose sight of the basic principles. Once you see the principles, we are confident you'll be able to apply them to your own, more complicated examples.

We have been selective in what we put into this book. Other books have useful and insightful things to say on the subject of design by contract, but we have concentrated on what makes this book different—the advice it gives on how to write good contracts.

And, of course, this book is not the end of the story of design by contract. There is more work to be done on writing contracts, on developing the underlying technology and the underlying theory, on applying the ideas in broader contexts, and on assessing the benefits in practice.

WEB SITE

There is a Web site associated with the book (http://www.awl.com/cseng/titles/0-201-63460-0/). It contains the source code of the examples. Our hope is that you will download the code and play with it. Change the code. Add bugs, both in the implementation and in the contracts, and see what happens. Change the examples into new ones. Experiment. Use them on real projects. That's how we learned about contracts.

ACKNOWLEDGMENTS

Many individuals contributed to this book. Bertrand Meyer deserves first mention. Bertrand gave us both Design by Contract and Eiffel to play with, and we hugely enjoyed playing with them. He continually encouraged our work on contracts and our efforts to put our findings into book form.

Reto Kramer developed the iContract tool, which allowed us to try out examples in Java. Reto also helped translate Eiffel examples into Java/iContract, which we discuss in Chapter 11. Chris Thomas developed a prototype preprocessor to add quantifiers to Eiffel's assertion language, which we use in Chapter 7.

We have benefited from working with many people in the field of contracts, and we have had many helpful comments from reviewers of earlier versions of this book. We would like to say thank you to all of them for their help: Jim Armstrong, Vladimir Bacvanski, Richie Bielak, Roger Browne, Christopher Creel, Roger Duke, John Howse, Ali Hamie, Brian Henderson-Sellers, Jean-Marc Jézéquel, Ian Maung, Christine Mingins, Agnes Mitchell, David Mondou, Roger Osmond, Bob Streich, Chris Thomas, Ted Velkoff, Richard Wiener, Jean-Francois Zubillaga, and anonymous reviewers. If we've left anyone off the list, please put it down to imperfect memories, forgive us, and assume that we are, nevertheless, very grateful.

We are grateful to the following institutions who supported us at one time or another while we were busy writing this book: InferData Corporation, Austin, Texas; Renssalaer at Hartford, Connecticut; Monash University, Melbourne, Australia; Brighton University, England.

Interactive Software Engineering, Inc., donated some of the Eiffel compilers we used to develop the examples, for which we thank them.

We apologize to our families for the time we spent writing rather than being husbands and fathers. Our thanks for their forbearance go to Agnes, James, Emma, Daniel, and Julia Mitchell; and to Mary, Krista, AJ, and Alex McKim.

Finally, each of us would like to thank the other for a very enjoyable and fruitful working partnership.

Richard Mitchell and Jim McKim

A First Taste of Design by Contract

1.1 ABOUT THIS CHAPTER

This chapter provides a quick introduction to design by contract. In doing so, it

- Shows you how contracts can specify the required behavior of a class, and how contracts can check the code at runtime.
- Explains that contracts are built of assertions, which are used to express preconditions, postconditions, and invariants. (Later chapters develop a small set of principles and guidelines to help you write high-quality contracts.)
- Provides an example that is a simplified version of what could be a real software component—a customer manager—but you don't need any experience with components to understand the example.
- Presents some of the benefits of design by contract, a theme that is followed up in more detail in Chapter 8.
- Offers a first taste of design by contract. It'll probably raise many questions in your mind. We haven't attempted to answer them all in Chapter 1. We hope the rest of the book will answer many of them.

Throughout this book we use the Unified Modeling Language (UML) for diagrams that summarize classes and the programming language Eiffel for writing contracts and implementations. (Chapter 11 presents two examples in Java.)

This book does not teach UML, Eiffel, or Java. We just explain the bits we need as we go along. The bibliography lists a small selection of books, papers, and Web sites where you can get more information.

1.2 THE CUSTOMER MANAGER EXAMPLE

The customer manager component explored here is, at its heart, a dictionary (also known as a directory or a look-up table), which is a classic, and basic, data structure. When we begin to develop principles and guidelines for designing with contracts, we deliberately use clean, simple, basic examples so as not to detract from the main message. For instance, Chapter 3 develops a contract for the DIC-TIONARY class. However, lessons learned from simple examples can be applied to realistic problems, such as customer manager components. We look at more complex examples toward the end of the book.

Let's imagine you are planning to use a software component that will manage all the information about your organization's customers. (The term "component" has many meanings. Components that manage a data resource are only one kind of component.)

An installed customer manager component has exclusive control over all customer objects. Figure 1.1 is a UML-style diagram showing extracts from the CUSTOMER_MANAGER and CUSTOMER types.

There is an association between these types. The black diamond tells us that customer objects are exclusively owned by a customer manager object. The asterisk tells us that a customer manager owns zero, one, or more customer objects.

The box for CUSTOMER_MANAGER lists the features you can use if you are a client of a customer manager object. (A feature is a method you can call or a public attribute you can inspect.) These features allow you to:

- Find out how many customers the manager owns. (The *count* feature might be implemented as a read-only attribute, or it might be made accessible through a *get_count()* method, depending on the implementation language.)
- Ask whether a particular customer id is active.

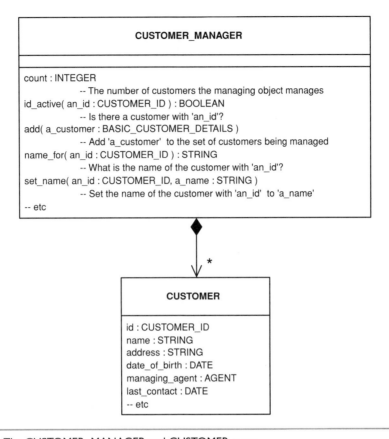

Figure 1.1 The CUSTOMER_MANAGER and CUSTOMER types

- Add a new customer to the customer manager component.

- Ask for the name of a customer whose id you know.

- Give an existing customer a new name.

The box for CUSTOMER lists some of the attributes of a customer (we do not need to explore the details of the methods).

The customer manager component has exclusive rights to modify customer objects, and clients of the component do not access customer objects directly. Instead, we provide some simpler types to allow clients to communicate with the

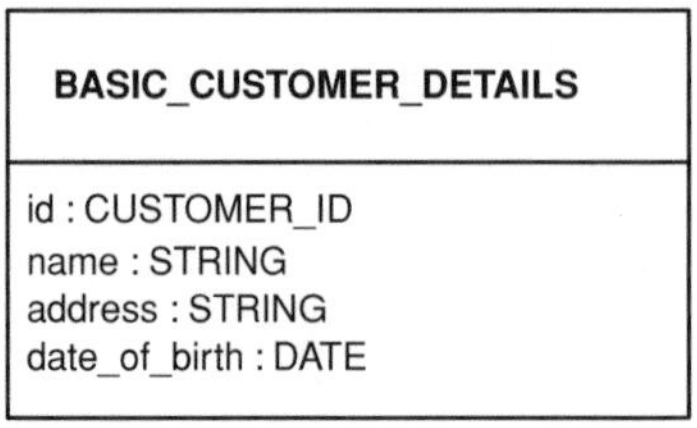

```
┌─────────────────────────────────────┐
│     BASIC_CUSTOMER_DETAILS           │
├─────────────────────────────────────┤
│  id : CUSTOMER_ID                    │
│  name : STRING                       │
│  address : STRING                    │
│  date_of_birth : DATE                │
└─────────────────────────────────────┘
```

Figure 1.2 The BASIC_CUSTOMER_DETAILS type

customer manager component about customer objects. Figure 1.2 shows just one of these simpler types, the BASIC_CUSTOMER_DETAILS type. This type allows a client to pass in the basic information needed to create a new customer object, for instance.

The basic details of a customer are an id (given to him or her by the bank), a name, an address, and a date of birth.

In Eiffel, attributes can be public, but then they are read-only. So the design in Figure 1.2 is also the Eiffel programmer's view. If we were programming in Java, for example, we would program it with the attributes and methods shown in Figure 1.3 (in the code, we'd make the Java attributes private, but we haven't shown that detail on the UML-style diagram).

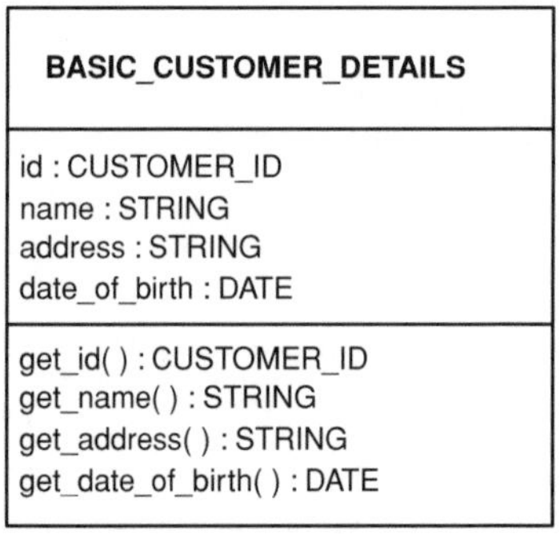

```
┌─────────────────────────────────────┐
│     BASIC_CUSTOMER_DETAILS           │
├─────────────────────────────────────┤
│  id : CUSTOMER_ID                    │
│  name : STRING                       │
│  address : STRING                    │
│  date_of_birth : DATE                │
├─────────────────────────────────────┤
│  get_id( ) : CUSTOMER_ID             │
│  get_name( ) : STRING                │
│  get_address( ) : STRING             │
│  get_date_of_birth( ) : DATE         │
└─────────────────────────────────────┘
```

Figure 1.3 A Java design for the BASIC_CUSTOMER_DETAILS type

In Eiffel syntax, the name of a customer would be given by *a_customer.name*. In Java syntax, it would be given by *a_customer.get_name()*.

The customer manager exclusively owns the customer objects, and only the customer manager can change the information about a customer, so there are no set methods in the BASIC_CUSTOMER_DETAILS class. If you do succeed in changing the state of a basic customer details object, this has no effect on the corresponding customer object that the customer manager owns. You have to call a method on the customer manager component in order to change anything about a customer object.

1.3   SOME QUESTIONS

Look again at the list of methods that a client of a customer manager can call.

count : INTEGER
        -- The number of customers the managing object manages
id_active(an_id : CUSTOMER_ID) : BOOLEAN
        -- Is there a customer with 'an_id'?
add(a_customer : BASIC_CUSTOMER_DETAILS)
        -- Add 'a_customer' to the set of customers being managed
name_for(an_id : CUSTOMER_ID) : STRING
        -- What is the name of the customer with 'an_id'?
set_name(an_id : CUSTOMER_ID, a_name : STRING)
        -- Set the name of the customer with 'an_id' to 'a_name'

As you design your client of the customer manager, here are some questions you might want answered.

- How do I make an id active? By adding a customer with that id?
- If I add a customer whose details match an existing customer's basic details, what happens?
- What do I get if I ask for the name of a customer whose id is not active?
- What happens if I set the name for a customer whose id is not active?

In a component world, the person who developed the component might work for a company on the other side of the globe—and might be sleeping peacefully when you want your questions answered! The component must come with documentation that answers your questions. In the next section, we show how a contract can provide the answers to your questions. In later chapters, we'll see how to write good contracts.

1.4 A Contract for CUSTOMER_MANAGER

The contract for the customer manager component contains smaller contracts, one for each of the features of the component. (Reminder: For now, a feature is a method or a public, read-only attribute. Sometimes we'll be lazy and talk of "calling a feature," even when we're actually inspecting an attribute.)

We'll explore these smaller contracts one by one. We hope you will concentrate on understanding each contract—don't worry yet about how to write a contract. And keep in mind that we are working on just a fragment of a component (so, for example, we will not discuss how the component is initialized).

By the end of this section, you'll know roughly what a contract is because you'll have seen an example: a contract is a collection of assertions (things that ought to be true) that describe precisely what each feature of the component does and doesn't do.

Adding a New Customer Here is the contract for the feature you use to add a customer to a customer manager component. It's followed by an explanation.

add(a_customer : BASIC_CUSTOMER_DETAILS)
        -- Add 'a_customer' to the set of customers
    require
        id_not_already_active:
            not *id_active(a_customer.id)*
    ensure
        count_increased:
            count = **old** *count + 1*

> customer_id_now_active:
>   *id_active(a_customer.id)*

The first line is a *signature*, which names the feature and lists its arguments (here we have just one argument, *a_customer*). The second line is a comment, which informally describes the feature.

The third line contains the keyword **require**, which introduces a *precondition*. A precondition is a condition that a client must be sure is true; otherwise, it is not legal for the client to call the feature (we'll explore later what happens if a client makes an illegal call). On the next line, the identifier *id_not_already_active* is a tag, or label, chosen by the programmer to improve readability (and to help with debugging—as we will see later). The precondition's assertion is in the next line, and says:

> **not** *id_active(a_customer.id)*

This asserts that, for it to be legal to call the *add* feature to add *a_customer*, it must *not* be true that the *id* of *a_customer* is an active id (we will soon know what makes an id active). The assertion is in Eiffel code so that it can be evaluated at runtime to check whether the client is keeping to its side of the contract.

The keyword **ensure** introduces a *postcondition*. A postcondition is a condition that should become true when the feature is executed (otherwise there is a bug in the code that implements the *add* feature).

In this example, the postcondition contains two assertions, each with its own tag. The first asserts that adding a customer increases the *count* by one. The expression **old** *count* is the value of the *count* before the feature was called. The = operator is the equality test, not the assignment operator. Asserting that the *count* now is what it was before, plus one, asserts that it has been increased by one.

The second assertion of the postcondition asserts that the *id* of the customer passed as argument is now active. This assertion, taken together with the precondition, says that you cannot add a customer if that customer's *id* is already active, and adding a customer makes that customer's *id* active.

Now we know the answers to the first two questions we asked earlier.

- How do I make an id active? By adding a customer with that id?

Yes.

- If I add a customer whose details match an existing customer's details, what happens?

You are not allowed to add a customer whose id equals the id of a customer already owned by the manager. If you keep to this rule, there are no further constraints on whether the name, address, and date of birth can be the same as those of an existing customer.

Setting the Name of a Customer Here is the contract for the feature you use to set the name of a customer.

```
set_name( an_id : CUSTOMER_ID; a_name : STRING )
        -- Set the name of the customer with 'an_id' to 'a_name'
    require
        id_active:
            id_active( an_id )
    ensure
        name_set:
            name_for( an_id ).is_equal( a_name )
```

The signature tells us that the feature takes a CUSTOMER_ID and a STRING as arguments.

The precondition (introduced by **require**) makes it illegal to try to set the name of a customer with *an_id* that is not active. In other words, it is illegal to try to change the name of a customer that has not been added to the customer manager.

The postcondition (introduced by **ensure**) asserts that if you now look up the name for the customer with *an_id*, you'll get back a name that is equal to *a_name*, the second argument to the *set_name* feature. In other words, if you set the name of a customer, that's the name the customer now has.

A small detail: Because strings are objects, we assert that we get back a string that *is_equal* to the name we passed in as argument. One string *is_equal* to another if they both contain the same characters in the same order. If we'd used the = operator, we would be asserting that we actually get back the string object we passed in. That would be overspecification.

Asking for the Name of a Customer   Here is the contract for the query feature *name_for*.

name_for(an_id : CUSTOMER_ID) : STRING
        -- The name of the customer with 'an_id'
    require
       id_active:
          id_active(an_id)

This time, there is only a precondition, which states that you must not ask for the name for a customer whose id is not active. Why is there no postcondition? Because you are told the value of this query feature in the postcondition of the *set_name* feature, the feature that defines the value that *name_for* should have.

Now you know the answers to the third and fourth of your questions.

- What do I get if I ask for the name of a customer whose id is not active?

  It is illegal to ask for the name of a customer whose id is not active.

- What happens if I set the name for a customer whose id is not active?

  It is illegal to attempt to set the name of a customer whose id is not active.

1.5   THE STORY SO FAR

Here, in one place, is the contract on the CUSTOMER_MANAGER component, followed by some discussion. There is a new part to the contract, an invariant.

The invariant asserts that *count* is always zero or greater. An *invariant* property of a component is always true (more precisely, it is true whenever you can call a feature on the component).

component *CUSTOMER_MANAGER*

 count : INTEGER
   -- The number of customers

 id_active(an_id : CUSTOMER_ID) : BOOLEAN
   -- Is there a customer with 'an_id'?

 add(a_customer : BASIC_CUSTOMER_DETAILS)
   -- Add 'a_customer' to the set of customers
  require
   id_not_already_active:
    not id_active(a_customer.id)
  ensure
   count_increased:
    count = **old** count + 1
   customer_id_now_active:
    id_active(a_customer.id)

 name_for(an_id : CUSTOMER_ID) : STRING
   -- The name of the customer with 'an_id'
  require
   id_active:
    id_active(an_id)

 set_name(an_id : CUSTOMER_ID; a_name : STRING)
   -- Set the name of the customer with 'an_id' to 'a_name'
  require
   id_active:
    id_active(an_id)
  ensure
   name_set:
    name_for(an_id).is_equal(a_name)

 ...

invariant

    count_never_negative:

        count $>= 0$

end

The contract is definitely unfinished. It still leaves many questions unanswered, but we hope you can see that a contract *can* answer many of the questions that a client programmer might ask.

The syntax of the component contract is that of the programming language Eiffel (except for the first line—Eiffel doesn't have special syntax to distinguish a component from a class).

The features *count* and *id_active* have neither preconditions nor postconditions. They don't have preconditions because it is always legal to call them. They don't have postconditions because their values are defined elsewhere. Specifically, the postcondition on the *add_customer* feature defines that *add_customer* both increments the *count* and makes *id_active* for the id of the added customer.

Notice how different parts of the component and its contract cannot be discussed in isolation. For example, the name returned by the *name_for* query feature is defined in the postcondition of the *set_name* feature. We cannot define the *name_for* some id without discussing the feature that sets it. Conversely, we cannot define what name is set for a customer by *set_name* without discussing the *name_for* query that tells us the name for the particular customer.

That's why we say that the component has a single contract (which, in turn, is made up of the individual contracts on the individual features).

1.6 RUNTIME CHECKING

So far, we have concentrated on the role that contracts play in specifying the behavior of a component. In this role, contracts are intended to be read by people. But contracts can also be checked at runtime. In this section, we'll see one example of what happens if you write careful contracts and then accidentally introduce bugs into the code. You might not be convinced by the example because it is so simple. More powerful examples of the benefits appear in later chapters.

Suppose, for example, that we got confused about the precise meaning of the *add* feature and believed that we could use it to change the details associated with an existing customer. Suppose we called *add* with a customer details argument whose *id* was already active. In a programming environment that understands contracts, we would be told something like the following (we'll assume the CUSTOMER_MANAGER component has been implemented by a class of the same name):

Stopped in **object** *[0xE96978]*
Class: *CUSTOMER_MANAGER*
Feature: *add*
Problem: *Precondition violated*
Tag: *id_not_already_active*
Arguments:
    a_customer: BASIC_CUSTOMER_DETAILS [0xE9697C]
Call stack:

                  CUSTOMER_MANAGER add
    was called by   *CUSTOMER_MANAGER_UIF change_customer*

This is the level of detail provided by the Eiffel development environment supplied by Interactive Software Engineering, Inc. Other environments provide similar detail (including other Eiffel environments and environments that add design by contract facilities to other programming languages, such as Java and C++). Working through this wealth of debugging information line by line, we can tell

1. That the application has stopped in some object (we could open the object with an object browser and examine its attributes).

2. That this object is of the class CUSTOMER_MANAGER.

3. That a problem arose when that class's *add* feature was called.

4. That the problem was that some part of the precondition on *add* was violated.

5. That if a precondition is violated, it means some client called the *add* feature when it was not legal to do so. Specifically, it was the part of the precondition with the *id_not_already_active* tag that was violated.

6. Which BASIC_CUSTOMER_DETAILS object was passed as an argument to the call.

7. The sequence of calls that led up to the problem: A *change_customer* feature in a *CUSTOMER_MANAGER_UIF* class (the user interface to the customer manager application) called the *add* feature in the CUSTOMER_MANAGER class.

Putting all this information together leads us to conclude that the *change_customer* feature in CUSTOMER_MANAGER_UIF class is the cause of the problem—it called *add* with a BASIC_CUSTOMER_DETAILS object whose id was already active, and the contract says that's illegal. In other words, the *change_customer* feature contains a bug, which we must find and fix.

Developers who make good use of contracts come to expect this amount of help when something goes wrong. They don't spend long hours hunting for the causes of a runtime error. They put their effort into writing contracts instead. And, in return, they get a second benefit, trustworthy documentation, which is the subject of the next section.

Just before we leave this section, though, we should explain that you might want contracts checked while you are developing an application, but you might not want production code to be slowed down by all this checking. In a programming environment that supports design by contract, you can turn contract-checking on and off. You can turn it on in some classes and off in others. And you can turn it on at different levels, such as checking only preconditions, rather than full checking of preconditions, postconditions, and invariants.

1.7   TRUSTWORTHY DOCUMENTATION

In the previous section, we saw that contracts can be checked at runtime, delivering valuable debugging information. We took an example of a faulty caller who broke a precondition. What if the component itself contains a bug? Then a postcondition (or the invariant) will evaluate to false, highlighting the problem and its cause.

For example, suppose that the developer of the component forgot to increment the *count* in the feature to *add* a new customer. During testing, the *add* feature is called. Its postcondition is evaluated. And up comes a message, like the one in the previous section, telling the developer that the false postcondition was the one with the tag *count_increased* in the *add* feature in the CUSTOMER_ MANAGER class.

If an application survives execution without any false preconditions, postconditions, or invariants, we can be sure that the code is doing what the contract says.

Now turn that around. By checking that the code is doing what the contract says, the runtime system is also checking that the documentation accurately says what the code does. If one assertion in the contract did not correctly describe what the code did, that assertion would evaluate to false on some test.

In other words, if you document your classes using contracts, you get documentation that everyone can trust to be telling the truth. There's a novelty!

Further, the documentation sets out clearly the rights and obligations of each party to the contract. In any one call to a feature, one object will be playing the role of client, or caller. The other will be playing the role of supplier.

A client calling a feature on a supplier has an *obligation* to fulfill the precondition. A client who calls a feature when its precondition is false has broken the client's side of the contract. The supplier's called feature has an *obligation* to terminate with the postcondition true. A feature that leaves its postcondition false has broken the supplier's side of the contract.

In return for these obligations, both parties obtain rights. The client has the *right* to expect that the called feature makes its postcondition true. If the postcondition is false, this is not the fault of the client. The supplier has the *right* to expect that the precondition is true. If the feature is called with the precondition false, this is not the fault of the supplier, which is then not obliged to meet its postcondition.

There is more on this theme in Chapter 8.

1.8   SUMMARY

Using a very simple example of (part of) a customer manager component, we've introduced the idea that a program can contain assertions. These assertions can be used to write preconditions, postconditions, and invariants.

A precondition specifies the circumstances under which it is valid to call a feature. A postcondition specifies the effect of calling a feature. An invariant specifies unchanging properties of the objects of a class.

Assertions can be checked at runtime to help us test and debug the implementation. As an important by-product of this checking, the documentation accurately describes what the code actually does.

Assertion-checking is built into Eiffel. For other languages such as Java and C++ you can obtain preprocessors that generate the code to turn your assertions into runtime checks, thereby getting the same benefits: runtime checking and trustworthy documentation. (In Chapter 11, we present examples that use the iContract tool developed by Reto Kramer, available from Trusted Systems.)

1.9   AN AIDE MEMOIRE

Contracts are "specs 'n' checks."

1.10   THINGS TO DO

In later chapters, we invite you to download (or rewrite) code and try using contracts for yourself, but this chapter did not present a complete example. However, we do have some suggestions for things you might do.

1. Start work on obtaining a programming environment in which you can try out contracts (download and install an Eiffel compiler, or seek a design by contract preprocessor for another language). This book makes a whole lot more sense if you play with contracts.

2. Choose an API (such as those you find in class libraries) and ask yourself what questions you cannot answer with certainty from the signatures and comments in the API. Where do you have to go for the answers? Would you like to get future libraries from a supplier who writes contracts? Would you pay extra for such libraries?

3. Browse the Web for information on design by contract. Quite a lot is out there. (See the bibliography for some Web sites that might help.)

We've deliberately built in lots of repetition of the concepts throughout the book. If you don't get an idea straight off, don't worry. It'll almost certainly come around again soon, and maybe its explanation will click then.

Elementary Principles of Design by Contract

2.1 ABOUT THIS CHAPTER

This chapter introduces six principles of design by contract. In doing so, it

- Uses a simple stack class as an example.
- Demonstrates that problems arise when we try to write contracts for the stack class, and that this motivates us to search for a set of principles to follow when developing contracts.
- Illustrates that the principles cover how to prepare a class for writing contracts and how to write the contracts themselves.
- Shows that applying the principles improves the contracts for the simple stack class. (Section 1.8 has a listing of the final version of the contracts on the stack class.)
- Teaches you enough to be able to write very thorough contracts on many classes.

The next three chapters consolidate the ideas presented in this chapter by applying the six principles to two new classes, a dictionary class and a queue class. The principles (and some supporting guidelines) are printed inside the front and back covers.

2.2 STACKS

We've chosen stacks for the example in this chapter because they are complicated enough that they raise some interesting issues, but simple enough that we don't need to introduce too many ideas at one time.

Figure 2.1 is a UML-style class diagram showing a design for a very simple version of a stack class.

The class is called *STACK*. It is a generic, or template, class. The generic parameter is class *G*. You can replace *G* by *INTEGER* to get a stack of integers; you can replace *G* by *TOKEN* to get a stack of tokens; and so on.

You can ask a stack object for a *count* of how many items it currently contains, and whether it *is_empty*.

The features *count* and *is_empty* are queries. The other features are commands— they change the state of a stack object.

You can *initialize* a newly created stack to be empty (or re-initialize an existing one). You can *push* an item *g* onto a stack. You can take it off again using *pop*, which has an **out** parameter in which to return the item popped.

In the rest of this chapter, we're going to develop contracts to specify the features in the STACK class, and we will meet six important principles of writing contracts along the way.

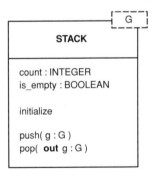

Figure 2.1 A very simple stack class

2.3   SEPARATE COMMANDS AND QUERIES

As soon as we start to write contracts for the STACK class, we'll discover it is better if we separate commands and queries more carefully than in the design shown in the previous section.

Consider the *push* operation. It takes an argument called *g*, and its effect is to place *g* on the top of the stack. Here's a first attempt at a postcondition for *push*.

push(g : G)
        -- Push 'g' onto the top of the stack
    ensure
        top_is_g:
            $g = ???$

At the point marked "???" we need an expression to say that *g* is the top item on the stack. We can inspect what is on top of the stack by calling *pop*. But *pop* doesn't return a result. It has an **out** parameter instead. We want a function so that we can talk about the result of a *pop*.

Let's redesign *pop* as a function.

pop : G
        -- Remove top item and return it

This is not a pure function because it changes the stack as well as returns a result. Here is the postcondition on *push*, rewritten to use the new version of *pop*.

push(g : G)
        -- Push 'g' onto the top of the stack
    ensure
        top_is_g:
            $g = pop$

This postcondition has a serious problem. Evaluating it changes the stack. Every time a client calls *push* to push some item *g* onto the stack, the postcondition is evaluated to check that all is well, and *pop* immediately removes the item *g* from the stack. So even though the postcondition will evaluate to true, it isn't the postcondition we want!

The solution is to split *pop* into two parts: one part tells us what is on the top of a stack (but doesn't delete it), and the other deletes what is on the top (but doesn't tell us what it was). Here are the signatures of the two new features.

top : G
      -- The item on the top of the stack
delete
      -- Delete the item on the top of the stack

Now we can specify the effect of a *push*.

push(g : G)
      -- Push 'g' onto the top of the stack
    ensure
      top_is_g:
        top = g

So, the first principle of writing contracts is to distinguish very carefully between commands and queries. Commands can change the state of an object but do not return a result. Queries return a result but do not change the state of an object. Commands are implemented as procedures. Queries are implemented as pure functions or as attributes. We need queries to write the assertions in the contracts. (A detail: If you write a function that returns a result and *also* changes the state of the object, it won't qualify as being a query.)

A reminder about attributes in Eiffel—if you leave an attribute public, clients can read the attribute but they cannot assign to it. Therefore, it is common practice to leave attributes public in Eiffel programs. This means that you do not need any *getAttribute* methods.

Figure 2.2 shows one way of looking at the relationship between commands and queries, and the attributes, functions, and procedures used to implement them.

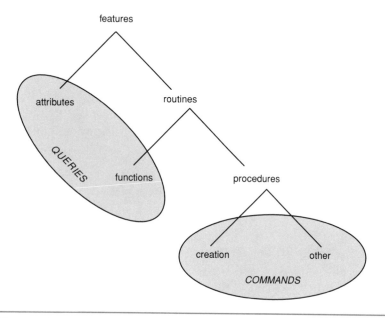

Figure 2.2 Commands and queries, and how they are implemented

Features are either attributes or routines. Some routines are functions (from now on, we'll use functions that are well behaved and don't change the state of an object). Together, the attributes and functions are the class's queries.

The other routines, the ones that are not functions, are procedures. Some can be used to initialize newly created objects, and some cannot. Together, they make up the commands that a client can issue to an object.

From now on, we will follow this first principle of designing contract.

> **PRINCIPLE 1   Separate commands and queries.** Queries return a result but do not change the visible properties of the object. Commands might change the object but do not return a result.

Do you remember the first version of the *pop* feature we encountered at the start of this chapter? It did two things: it removed the top item from the stack, and it returned this top item in an **out** parameter. Adding an **out** parameter to a feature is another way to make it return a result. So we would say that *pop(**out** g : G)* is neither a pure query (because it modifies the stack) nor a pure command (because it returns a result in an **out** parameter).

On some occasions, you may really need a feature that is a mixture of a command and a query. These two versions of the *pop* feature are both mixtures.

- *pop(**out** g : G)* removes the top item from the stack and returns a result in its **out** parameter.
- *pop : G* removes the top item from the stack and returns a result directly.

If you do need such mixed features, we recommend that you also provide the more primitive command and query features of which it is a mixture and specify the mixed feature in terms of these simpler primitives.

2.4 NAMING CONVENTIONS

The Eiffel libraries from Interactive Software Engineering, Inc., are designed around several conventions, including a naming convention. This naming convention was thought out over several years, and we will adopt it here.

Our first application of the convention results in the renaming of some of the features of the stack class.

In the general world of programming, you know what method to call to add an item to a stack—it's the *push* method. You might guess that *append* adds an item to a queue. But what about adding an item to a sequence, a dictionary, a hash table, and so on? One approach is always to name the method *put*. When you call *put* on a stack, you put an item on top of the stack (because that's how stacks work). When you call *put* on a queue, you put an item at the end of the queue (because that's how queues work). It's a little strange, at first, using *put* to push an item onto a stack, but the benefit is that now you know the name of the method used to put items into any one of a large library of container classes.

Similarly, *remove* is the standard name for deleting from a container, respecting the properties of the container. When you *remove* from a stack, you remove the most recently added object. When you *remove* from a queue, you remove the oldest object.

The standard query on containers is called *item*. For a stack, this is the item on the top of the stack, whereas, for a queue, *item* is the item at the head of the queue.

You have already met two other conventions.

- *count* is the standard name for the number of items in a container.
- Boolean queries have names that invite a *yes* or *no* answer (we have met *is_empty*).

We do break the convention at one point. The standard name for a routine that initializes a newly created object is *make*. Strictly, the object is made by the runtime system. The code we write to help construct an object initializes the properties of the object once it has been made. We will use the name *initialize* for a feature that can be used to initialize a newly created object.

Figure 2.3 shows how the stack class looks after separating the commands from the queries and applying the naming conventions. We've taken the opportunity to rename the whole class *SIMPLE_STACK*, to distinguish it from the *STACK* class in the Eiffel library, which has several additional features that we will not look at in this chapter.

2.5   SEPARATE BASIC QUERIES AND DERIVED QUERIES

Clients can ask a stack if it *is_empty*. They can also ask for a *count* of the number of items on the stack. These two queries are, of course, related. A stack is empty when it contains zero items. Conversely, if it contains one or more items, it is not empty. We can capture the relationship in a postcondition on the *is_empty* feature.

is_empty : BOOLEAN
      -- Does the stack contain no items?
  ensure
      consistent_with_count:
         Result = (count = 0)

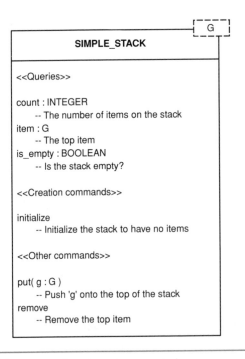

Figure 2.3 Stack class with its commands and queries separated

The tag reminds readers that the result of the *is_empty* query must be consistent with the current value of the *count*. The formal assertion says that the *Result* of calling *is_empty* is the same as asking whether *count* is equal to zero. (*Result* is a built-in variable that holds the result that a function will return to its caller.)

By specifying *is_empty* in terms of *count*, we have made it easier to define the contracts on other features. For example, if we define that *put* increments the *count*, we don't also have to say it makes *is_empty* false. That can be inferred from the contract on *is_empty*.

From now on, we will also follow the second and third principles of designing contracts.

> **P**RINCIPLE 2   **Separate basic queries from derived queries.**
> Derived queries can be specified in terms of basic queries.

> **P**RINCIPLE 3   **For each derived query, write a postcondition that specifies what result will be returned in terms of one or more basic queries.** Then, if we know the values of the basic queries, we also know the values of the derived queries.

By recognizing that *is_empty* is a derived query, we are following Principle 2. And by specifying the postcondition on *is_empty* in terms of *count,* we are following Principle 3.

Figure 2.4 gives another overview of the *SIMPLE_STACK* class, this time with basic queries separated from derived ones.

The story isn't finished yet. In the next section, we will find a reason to change our minds about defining *item* as a basic query. (Reminder: *item* is Eiffel's name for *top.*)

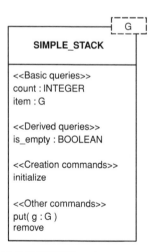

Figure 2.4 Class stack with basic and derived queries distinguished

2.6 SPECIFY HOW COMMANDS AFFECT BASIC QUERIES

In this section, we specify how each command affects the basic queries. We explain now why we want to do that, and we'll explain it again later in the section.

If we can specify the effect each command has on the basic queries, our specifications will be very thorough. What you can know about an object is what you can ask it via its queries. Once you know the values of the basic queries, you can work out the values of the derived queries, provided Principle 3 has been followed. So, all we have to do is specify the effect of each command on the basic queries, and all the questions you could ask about a stack will have answers. That's what we mean when we say that the contracts will be very thorough specifications.

Let's try this approach for *put*, then *initialize*, and finally *remove*.

The *put* Command   The *put* command has an effect on the *count*. Specifically, it increases the *count* by one. It also has an effect on the top *item*. After a *put*, the top of the stack must be the *item* that was just put. We can express these facts as assertions in a postcondition on *put*, as shown here.

put(g : G)
           -- Push 'g' onto the top of the stack
     ensure
        count_increased:
            count = ***old*** *count + 1*
        g_on_top:
            item = *g*

The postcondition contains two clauses, one to specify the effect on *count*, and one to specify the effect on the top *item*. In Eiffel, the assertions in the two clauses are treated as though there is a logical **and** between them. They must *both* be true for the postcondition to be satisfied.

The *initialize* Command   The *initialize* command is a little trickier to specify. The most obvious effect of calling *initialize* is to set the *count* to zero—there are no items on a stack that has just been created. The corresponding postcondition is easy to write.

initialize
　　　　-- Initialize the stack to be empty
　　ensure
　　　　stack_contains_zero_items:
　　　　　　count = 0

What can we say about the other basic query, *item*? We want to say that, if a stack is empty, it has no top *item*. How can we express that fact? To say that a stack has no top *item* is to say that it is not legal to call *item*. We can say that it is sometimes illegal to call *item* by giving *item* a precondition.

item
　　　　-- The top item on the stack
　　require
　　　　stack_not_empty:
　　　　　　count > 0

Now we'll bring two pieces of the specification together. The effect of *initialize* on *count* is to set it to zero (see the postcondition on *initialize*). The *item* query has no value when *count* is zero (see the precondition on *item*). Taken together, therefore, our contracts say that *initialize* ensures that

• The value of *count* is zero.
• The top *item* has no value.

In other words, our contracts have specified the effect of *initialize* on both the basic queries, *count* and *item*. We often need to construct short logical arguments about contracts, like the preceding one, in order to explain how they work together. That's natural in an object-oriented world. A class defines a set of features that work together on a common state. It would be surprising if we could specify them independently.

The *remove* Feature Now we turn to the *remove* feature, and here we discover a problem. The *remove* feature has two effects. It reduces the number of items by one, and it deletes the top *item*, uncovering an item pushed earlier. Of course, it cannot do either of these things when the stack is empty, so we can give it a precondition, just like the one for *item*. And we can easily write a postcondition that says that *remove* reduces the number of items by one.

remove
        -- Remove the top item
    require
        stack_not_empty:
            count > 0
    ensure
        count_decreased:
            *count = **old** count – 1*

Now all we have to do is specify that *remove* uncovers an earlier item. But we only have queries that refer to the *count* and the top *item*, the one being removed. We can't (yet) talk about earlier items.

We need to rethink our basic queries. We need a query that allows us to talk about the item that is on top of the stack now, and the one that was pushed before it (because that will be revealed when we do a *remove*), and the one that was pushed before that (because it will be revealed when we do another *remove*), and so on.

What we need is a query that allows us to talk about any of the items on a stack. We will introduce a suitable query and use it in writing contracts. In a later section, we'll try to take away any worries you might have about giving away the secrets of a stack.

Here is a query that allows us to talk about any of the items on a stack.

item_at(i : INTEGER) : G
        -- The item at logical position 'i' in the stack
        -- The oldest item is at position 1, and the
        -- top item is at position 'count'
    require
        i_large_enough:
            i >= 1
        i_small_enough:
            i <= count

The *item_at(i)* query returns the item at logical position *i* on the stack (the result is of type *G*). Position one is where you'll find the oldest item, the one that would be removed last. Position *count* is where you'll find the youngest item, the one that would be removed first. The two assertions in the precondition make sure that *item_at* is only called with values of *i* between one and *count,* inclusive.

The item at position *count* is the youngest item, so it is the top *item* on the stack. Therefore, we can define the top *item* in terms of *item_at(count)*. In other words, *item* is no longer one of our basic queries because it can be derived from *item_at*. Applying Principle 3, we write a postcondition to specify the result of *item* in terms of *item_at* (with a precondition to guard against invalid calls to *item*).

item : G
        -- The top item on the stack
    require
        not_empty:
            count > 0
    ensure
        consistent_with_item_at:
            Result = item_at(count)

Figure 2.5 gives yet another overview of the stack class, this time with *count* and *item_at* as the basic queries, and *item* and *is_empty* as derived queries.

Having changed our minds about what the basic queries are, we need to go back to each of the commands and rewrite their postconditions. Each command must now specify what changes it makes to *count* and *item_at.*

The *put* Command Revisited The *put* command increases the *count* and puts its argument, *g*, on top of the stack. The top of the stack is always at position *item_at(count)*. Here's the new contract.

put(g : G)
        -- Push 'g' onto the top of the stack

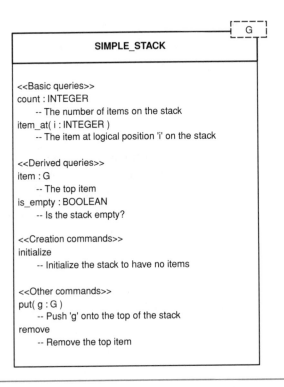

Figure 2.5 The class stack with new basic queries

ensure
  count_increased:
    count = **old** *count* + 1
  g_on_top:
    item_at(count) = g

The *initialize* Command Revisited The *initialize* command sets the *count* to zero. As a consequence, it makes it invalid to ask for an *item_at* any position on the stack—there aren't any items. Look again at the precondition on *item_at*.

item_at(i : INTEGER) : G
      -- The item at logical position 'i' in the stack
      -- The oldest item is at position 1, and the
      -- top item is at position 'count'

require
    i_large_enough:
        i >= 1
    i_small_enough:
        i <= count

When *count* is zero no values of *i* are valid because a valid *i* would have to be both greater than or equal to one *and* less than or equal to zero.

Once again, we have constructed a short logical argument to connect two contracts. We have shown that *initialize* does specify its effect on both the basic queries. Its postcondition says directly that it makes the *count* zero. This, together with the precondition on *item_at*, says that *initialize* makes it invalid to call *item_at* with any value of *i*. We can summarize the argument in a comment.

initialize
    -- Initialize the stack to be empty
  ensure
    stack_contains_zero_items:
        count = 0
    item_at_undefined:
        -- There are no values of 'i' for
        -- which 'item_at(i)' is defined

The *remove* Command Revisited   Here is the original version of the contract for *remove*.

remove
    -- Remove the top item
  require
    stack_not_empty:
        count > 0
  ensure
    count_decreased:
        *count = **old** count – 1*

The problem we had earlier was that the postcondition did not tell us what the new top value was. But now it does! As soon as we specify that the value of *count* has decreased, we know that the top *item* is a different one because the top *item* is always the *item_at(count)*. If *count* changes, so does the top *item*.

Summary We have carefully constructed contracts for our three commands so that each of them specifies its effect on the basic queries. We had to change our minds about what the basic queries were in order to achieve this goal. But having achieved it, we can now see that

- Every command specifies its effect on every basic query.
- Sometimes the specification is direct—the effect is captured in an assertion in the postcondition of the command (the effects of the *put, initialize,* and *remove* commands on the basic query *count* are good examples).
- Sometimes the specification is indirect. For example, *initialize* specifies that the *count* is zero. The precondition on *item_at* implies that there are then no valid values of *i* with which to call *item_at*. So, indirectly, *initialize* specifies its effect on *item_at*. It makes it invalid to call *item_at*.
- All the derived queries have postconditions that specify their results in terms of the basic queries.

Here's an example of how these contracts tell you what you need to know about a stack in order to use it. Consider the following fragment of a program that is a client of the SIMPLE_STACK class:

```
some_client_feature is
        -- Manipulate a simple stack
    local
        ss : SIMPLE_STACK[ INTEGER ]
    do
        create ss.initialize
        ss.put( 10 )
        ss.put( 20 )
        ss.put( 30 )
```

>   *ss.remove*
>   -- What's the top item at this point?
>   *end*

The feature declares a local variable that is a simple stack of integers (the compiler substitutes INTEGER for the generic parameter G). The first instruction has two parts:

- *create ss* creates a new object to attach to the variable *ss*. The type of the newly created object is *SIMPLE_STACK[INTEGER]*, to match the declaration of *ss*.
- *.initialize* calls the *initialize* routine on this newly created object, which sets the *count* to zero.

The next instruction puts 10 on the stack. From the postcondition on *put*, we can infer that the count goes up to 1 and that the *item_at(1)* is 10. Similarly, after *put(20)* we can infer that the *count* is 2 and the *item_at(2)* is 20. And after *put(30)*, we can infer that *count* is 3 and *item_at(3)* is 30.

Now comes an instruction to remove the top *item*. The postcondition of *remove* specifies that the count will go down to 2. We already know that the *item_at(2)* is 20. So the top *item* after the remove is 20.

We can summarize the way we have been writing postconditions on commands in this section in another principle.

> **P**RINCIPLE 4   **For each command, write a postcondition that specifies the value of every basic query.** Taken together with the principle of defining derived queries in terms of basic queries, this means that we now know the total visible effect of each command.

To be precise, we don't always follow this principle fully. When a command doesn't change the value of a basic query, we don't necessarily include an assertion to specify that the value did *not* change. We can extend our contracts to include assertions about properties that do not change. Such assertions are usually called frame rules. We address the topic of frame rules in Chapter 7.

Throughout this chapter, we have also been carefully following another principle, about preconditions.

> **P**RINCIPLE 5   **For every query and command, decide on a suitable precondition.** Preconditions constrain when clients may call the queries and commands.

For example, we had to get the precondition on *item_at* right in order to know how *item_at* was affected by *initialize*. We had to say that, when *count* is zero, there are no valid values of *i* for which *item_at(i)* is defined.

2.7   CAPTURE UNCHANGING PROPERTIES IN INVARIANTS

An invariant property of an object is an observable property that does not change throughout its lifetime. More precisely, an invariant property is a property that always has the same value whenever you are allowed to inspect that property.

For example, the *count* of the number of items on a stack goes up and down as clients *put* items on the stack and *remove* them again. But *count* has an unchanging property. It is always greater than or equal to zero (in other words, it is never negative).

We can do two things with this fact. We can construct a short argument to support it. And we can capture it formally in a class invariant.

Here is the argument that *count* is never negative. There is only one creation routine, *initialize*, and it sets *count* to zero (see the postcondition on *initialize*). Any subsequent call to *initialize* would re-initialize *count* to zero. Once it has been re-initialized, *count* can be changed by only two routines, *put* and *remove*. (They are the only commands whose postconditions assert that *count* can have a changed value.) The *put* routine increases *count*, so it remains non-negative. The *remove* routine reduces the *count*, but it has a precondition that the *count* is at least one. Therefore, *remove* can never decrease *count* below zero. Therefore, *count* can never be given a negative value.

Here is the invariant that records this fact.

invariant
    count_never_negative:
        count >= 0

The invariant helps readers to build the correct conceptual model of a stack. When you count items, the numbers you use are 0, 1, 2, ... Someone who thinks that the number of items on a stack could be, for instance, −3 has the wrong conceptual model of stacks and misunderstands the meaning of the *count* query.

Of course, because you are familiar with stacks, the invariant doesn't tell you much. But notice how we had to talk about all the commands in the class to argue that the invariant is correct. That means that the invariant captures a truly classwide concept. It also means that we've had to review all of our commands, so the process of formulating the invariant encourages us to carefully review the design of the class and its contract.

Now we have the last of our six principles.

PRINCIPLE 6 **Write invariants to define unchanging properties of objects.** Concentrate on properties that help the reader build an appropriate conceptual model of the abstraction that the class embodies.

A useful tip is to look for properties that cannot easily be deduced from the specification of any single feature, but require you to construct an argument about several features.

Of course, if you can deduce an invariant property from the contracts of the individual features, then, strictly speaking, the invariant is redundant. Should you include redundant assertions? Our answer is yes. An invariant that summarizes a logical argument concerning properties of several features confirms to the reader that his or her understanding of the interaction of the features is correct (or demonstrates that the understanding is faulty). That's often very helpful.

In fact, we would go further and say that, generally, invariants in classes should be deducible from the contracts on the individual features. (This general rule does not apply to abstract classes—classes that do not have instances—nor does it apply when we use an invariant to capture a postcondition on an attribute, which arises in Chapter 5.)

2.8   THE CLASS AND ITS CONTRACT

Here, in one place, is the contract-level view of the *SIMPLE_STACK* class. This is a prototype version, designed to be easy to implement. For example, there is no protection against overfilling a stack.

We should mention a few new things. The listing begins with an indexing clause, which gives an informal description of the class. The listing is headed *class interface* because it shows only the contracts, *not* the code that actually provides the implementation of STACK class. The keyword *creation* defines which commands can be used to initialize a newly created stack (in this case, only one, *initialize*). And finally, the keyword *feature* has been repeated several times so that we can record our categorization of the various queries and commands (you could do a similar thing in Java, for instance, by repeating the keyword *public*).

indexing
       description: "Simple version of stack, with few features and no protection against overfilling, but with carefully written contracts."

class interface
       SIMPLE_STACK [G]

creation
       initialize

feature -- 1. Basic queries

    count: INTEGER
          -- The number of items on the stack

    item_at (i: INTEGER): G
          -- The item at position 'i', where position
          -- 'count' is the top of the stack
    require
        i_big_enough: $i >= 1$;
        i_small_enough: $i <= count$

feature -- 2. Derived queries

    is_empty: BOOLEAN
          -- Does the stack contain no items?
    ensure
        consistent_with_count: *Result = (count = 0)*

    item: G
          -- The item on the top of the stack
    require
        stack_not_empty: *count > 0*
    ensure
        consistent_with_item_at:
            Result = item_at (count)

feature -- 3. Creation commands

    initialize
          -- Initialize the stack to be empty
    ensure
        stack_is_empty: *count = 0*

feature -- 4. Other commands

    put (g: G)
          -- Push 'g' onto the stack

> **ensure**
> count_increased: *count* = **old** *count* + 1;
> g_on_top: *item_at (count)* = *g*
>
> remove
> -- Delete the top item
> **require**
> stack_not_empty: *count* > 0
> **ensure**
> count_decreased: *count* = **old** *count* − 1
>
> *invariant*
> *count_is_never_negative: count* >= 0;
>
> **end** -- class SIMPLE_STACK

A tiny detail: The Eiffel tool we use to extract the preceding listing of the contract from a source code file has its own idea of how to order the sections. Our numbering scheme keeps the order we prefer when teaching people about contracts: first the basic queries, then the derived queries, then the creation commands, and finally the other commands.

2.9 THE BASIC QUERIES ARE A CONCEPTUAL MODEL OF STACKS

In this section, we look at the basic queries, especially the *item_at* query, and ask two complementary questions.

- What do the basic queries do for us?
- Should we be allowed to look at every item on a stack?

The Basic Queries Form a Conceptual Model   The answer to the question "What do the basic queries do for us?" is that they provide a conceptual model of objects of the class being specified. The two basic queries, *count* and *item_at*, give us a model of a stack object. We can show what we mean by presenting a more graphical model of an example stack object, with the values of the basic queries alongside.

In an earlier section, we talked about a client putting 10, 20, and then 30 onto a stack object. Figure 2.6 shows a picture of that stack and, alongside it, the values of the basic queries on the stack. The picture and the basic queries give us two models of the stack (one model is pictorial, the other textual).

Using the model provided by the basic queries, *count* and *item_at*, we can say all the things we want to say about a stack object. We can say

- What a stack looks like when it's just been initialized: *count* is zero and there are no items (because there are no values of *i* for which *item_at(i)* is valid).
- What the effect of *put(g)* is: *count* has increased and *g* is the *item_at(count)*.
- What the effect of *remove* is: *count* has decreased.
- What the result of *is_empty* is: it's the same as *count=0.*
- What the result of *item* is: it's the same as *item_at(count).*

If you try to write contracts on the features of the stack class with a weaker model, you'll find there are things you want to say but cannot. Do you remember, in an earlier section, we were using *count* and the top *item* as our basic queries, in other words, as our model? There we discovered we could not say that *remove* uncovered an item that had been pushed earlier.

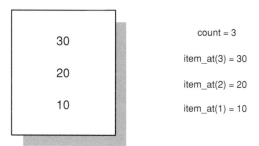

Figure 2.6 A picture of a stack and the values of the corresponding basic queries

We have devised a conceptual model of stacks. Stacks have an ordered set of items (*item_at(1)*, *item_at(2)*, *item_at(3)*, and so on), and we know how many items there are (that's what *count* tells us).

Further, we have made this conceptual model *explicit* in the design of the class. The class designer devises the model and uses it as the basis of the contracts that specify the features of the class. Whoever programs the stack can see the model and devise a suitable implementation model to represent it. Client programmers can see the model and the contracts it supports, and they can use them to learn what the various features of the stack class do.

We Are Not Revealing Any Secrets The answer to the question "Should we be allowed to look at every item on a stack?" is "Yes, it's okay. We are not revealing any secrets." We can show this with a small example of a program that is a client of class STACK.

The following imaginary client of a stack returns the item at position *i* in a stack. It doesn't use the feature we provided. It calculates the item at position *i* using features that are generally accepted to be part of the interface to a stack, namely, *count, remove,* and *item* (i.e., *top*).

class AN_INQUISITIVE_CLIENT

feature
    client_version_of_item_at(
        ss : SIMPLE_STACK[REAL];
        i : INTEGER) : REAL **is**
            -- The *item* at position *i* in the stack
       require
           i_is_large_enough:
               i >= 1
           i_small_enough:
               i <= ss.count
      local
           index : INTEGER

```
do
    from
        index := ss.count
    until
        index = i
    loop
        ss.remove
        index := index – 1
    end
    Result := ss.item
ensure
    ...
end
```

There is a precondition on the argument *i*. It must lie between 1 and the *count* of the number of items on the first argument, *ss*, a simple stack of real numbers. Then there is a declaration of a local variable, *index*, which is used as a loop variable. The body of the feature is introduced by the keyword *do*. It starts by setting *index* to the *count* of the number of items in the argument stack *ss*. It then loops (possibly zero times) until *index* is equal to the argument *i*. Each time around the loop it removes the top item from the stack. The *Result* the feature returns is whatever is then the top *item* of *ss*.

(It would be easy to improve this algorithm so that it kept the removed items on another stack and had the courtesy to put them back onto the original stack.)

As you will have noticed, the result that the feature returns is equal to *ss.item_at (position)*. What's important about the algorithm is that it can calculate *item_at* using only *count*, *remove*, and *item* (i.e., *top*), which are accepted features of a stack class. In other words, if you give me *count*, *remove*, and *item*, I can work out *item_at(i)* for myself. It is *not* a secret.

You could also think of it like this. Imagine a pile of books on a table. You could look at the pile to determine which is the third item from the bottom or the fifth item from the bottom. But, provided that you only put new books onto the top of the pile and only ever remove books from the top of the pile, the pile behaves exactly like a stack. It has the classic last-in, first-out behavior that characterizes a stack. Inspecting all the items on a stack does not destroy this essential characteristic behavior.

That's why we are not worried about providing the basic query *item_at* to clients. It provides a good model of stacks, which supports thorough contracts, and it does *not* give away any secrets.

It is important to understand that query *item_at(i)* does not reveal the implementation of the stack class. The implementation also needs a model, at a much more concrete level. For example, the stack class can be implemented using an array in which to hold the stacked items, or a linked list of nodes, each holding one item. But, even though the class provides the *item_at(i)* feature, you cannot find out how the stack is implemented.

Of course, we would not apply the same arguments to features such as *put_at(i)* or *remove_from(i)*. Such features would destroy the last-in, first-out property that is the essence of stacks. The difference is that *item_at(i)* is a query, whereas *put_at(i)* and *remove_from(i)* are commands.

2.10 THE SIX PRINCIPLES

Here are the six principles of design by contract introduced in this chapter.

> **PRINCIPLE 1   Separate queries from commands.** Queries return a result but do not change the visible properties of the object. Commands might change the object but do not return a result.

> **PRINCIPLE 2   Separate basic queries from derived queries.** Derived queries can be specified in terms of basic queries.

PRINCIPLE 3   For each derived query, write a postcondition that specifies what result will be returned in terms of one or more basic queries. Then, if we know the values of the basic queries, we also know the values of the derived queries.

PRINCIPLE 4   For each command, write a postcondition that specifies the value of every basic query. Now we know the total visible effect of each command.

PRINCIPLE 5   For every query and command, decide on a suitable precondition. Preconditions constrain when clients may call the queries and commands.

PRINCIPLE 6   Write invariants to define unchanging properties of objects. Concentrate on properties that help the reader build an appropriate conceptual model of the abstraction that the class embodies.

We haven't yet seen how to follow them to the letter. In particular, when we apply Principle 4, we concentrate on defining the *change* each command makes to the object. In Chapter 7 we will see how to go one step further and define what does *not* change, too.

2.11   THINGS TO DO

From the book's Web site, you can download the source code for a prototype implementation of SIMPLE_STACK class, together with a class that makes calls to its features. The implementation is based on an array. It is designed to be played with but not to be used in real programs.

If you don't have access to an Eiffel compiler, design an implementation for the SIMPLE_STACK class in some other language. Ideally, choose a language for which you can get a preprocessor for contracts. Then you can try these suggested exercises.

1. Compile and execute the demonstration program, or write your own version in a programming language for which you have support for contracts (e.g., Java and iContract—see the bibliography at the end of the book).

2. In some programs (for example, many real-time applications), it is safer to allocate space for containers statically, so that they do not change size at runtime. Extend the SIMPLE_STACK class to have a maximum capacity, as follows. Add an attribute *capacity*. Add an argument to the *initialize* routine to set the *capacity* when the stack is created. You'll want to constrain the argument with a precondition because a capacity of −3, for example, makes no sense (Principle 5). And you'll want to say how *initialize* sets the *capacity* in its postcondition (Principle 4). Introduce a derived query *is_full* with a postcondition (Principle 3). Give *put* a precondition that uses *is_full* (Principle 5).

3. Write a client that contains the *client_version_of_item_at* method from Section 2.9. The *client_version_of_item_at* method uses *count, item,* and *remove* to calculate the item at a given *position*. You can check that your implementation is correct by writing a postcondition on the method that checks that it really is delivering *ss.item_at(position)*.

4. Design a *replace* feature for the stack class, which replaces the top element. To design a feature you must choose its signature (name, arguments if any, return type if any) and devise a precondition and a postcondition. Because *replace* is a command, pay particular attention to Principle 4.

5. Implement your *replace* feature, and test that its assertions do not evaluate to false at runtime.

6. Design a *get_item* feature that both removes the top element and returns it to the client (to understand the name, think of getting a plate from a stack of plates). Having such a feature is a violation of Principle 1, but sometimes that's necessary. For example, perhaps you're building a distributed system,

and the overhead of calling *remove* and *item* separately over a network is too great. Follow the other five principles in your design.

7. Implement the *get_item* feature, and test it.

8. In any of your examples, deliberately plant bugs in the implementation code and explore how the contracts detect the bugs. Can you find bugs that the contracts cannot detect? (Hint: What if a stack kept a secret copy of every pushed item in some other object?)

Applying the Six Principles

3.1 ABOUT THIS CHAPTER

This chapter applies the six principles to a DICTIONARY class. In doing so, it

- Defines a dictionary as a container that holds keys, each with an associated value. (The customer manager from Chapter 1 is, at heart, a kind of dictionary.)
- Introduces new features, which usually happens as we devise the contract for a class we haven't worked on before.
- Constructs arguments about how individual contracts on several features work together, which is an important part of devising contracts.
- Introduces the first of several guidelines that augment the six principles (this one suggests using preconditions to guard against null arguments).

3.2 DICTIONARIES

A dictionary holds keys, and for each key it also holds a value. For example, a dictionary could hold people's names as the keys and people's e-mail addresses as the associated values.

You can think of a dictionary as a look-up table. When you have put a key and an associated value into the dictionary, you can look up the value for that key. The name "dictionary" comes from thinking about language dictionaries, which contain headwords (keys) and definitions of these words (values associated with keys).

These features provide the essential functionality of a dictionary.

initialize
    -- Initialize a dictionary to be empty
put (k: KEY; v: VALUE)
    -- Put key 'k' into the dictionary with associated value 'v'
value_for (k: KEY): VALUE
    -- The value associated with key 'k'
remove (k: KEY)
    -- Remove key 'k' from the dictionary

So far, we have given signatures for the features and informal descriptions of what they do. We are ready to begin writing contracts for these features, applying our six principles.

3.3 SEPARATING AND CATEGORIZING FEATURES

The first two of our six principles concern separating features into different categories.

> **PRINCIPLE 1 Separate queries from commands.** Queries return a result but do not change the visible properties of the object. Commands might change the object but do not return a result.

> **PRINCIPLE 2 Separate basic queries from derived queries.** Derived queries can be specified in terms of basic queries.

Of the features introduced earlier, *value_for* is a query. If there is only one query, there cannot be any derived queries. The other features are all commands. Of these, *initialize* is intended to be a creation routine—when a dictionary object is created, *initialize* puts it into a defined initial state.

We can write the following outline design for the class. It has one basic query, one creation command, and two other commands. It is generic in the kinds of keys and values it can hold. We will add more features when we write the contracts.

class DICTIONARY [KEY, VALUE]

creation
    initialize

feature -- 1. Basic queries

    value_for (k: KEY): VALUE
           -- The value associated with key 'k'

feature -- 2. Creation commands

    initialize
           -- Initialize a dictionary to be empty

feature -- 3. Other commands

    put (k: KEY; v: VALUE)
           -- Put key 'k' into the dictionary with associated value 'v'

    remove (k: KEY)
           -- Remove key 'k' from the dictionary

end -- class DICTIONARY

3.4 Postconditions

The next two principles are about writing postconditions.

> **PRINCIPLE 3** **For each derived query, write a postcondition that specifies what result will be returned, in terms of one or more basic queries.** Now, if we know the values of the basic queries, we also know the values of the derived queries.

> **PRINCIPLE 4** **For each command, write a postcondition that specifies the value of every basic query.** Then we know the total visible effect of each command.

Because we have no derived queries, Principle 3 does not apply. By Principle 4, we need to write postconditions on the three commands, and each postcondition must specify how it changes the value of the basic query, which in our case is *value_for*. We will look at *put*, then *initialize*, then *remove*.

The *put* Command   When a key *k* has been *put* into a dictionary with value *v*, the *value_for(k)* should be *v*. We can express this in the postcondition on *put*.

```
put (k: KEY; v: VALUE)
        -- Put key 'k' into the dictionary with associated value 'v'
    ensure
        value_for_k_is_v:
            value_for( k ) = v
```

The *remove* Command   When a key *k* has been removed from a dictionary, it is no longer there to be looked up. There is no *value_for(k)* anymore—it makes no sense to call *value_for(k)*. The way to say that "it makes no sense to call feature

X" is to give feature X an appropriate precondition. Informally, the precondition on *value_for* must say something like this:

> "If key *k* has never been put in the dictionary, or it has been put in but has since been removed, you can't ask for the value for key *k.*"

To turn this into a formal assertion, we need a way to talk about whether a key has been put into a dictionary, and whether it has since been removed. A query to ask whether a dictionary *has* a certain key will do the job.

A New Query, *has* If a key has been *put* into a dictionary, the dictionary now *has* that key. Here is a basic query on dictionaries to test whether a given key is in the dictionary.

has (k: KEY): BOOLEAN
        -- Does the dictionary contain key 'k'?

Here is how we can use it in the postcondition on *put*.

put (k: KEY; v: VALUE)
        -- Put key 'k' into the dictionary with associated value 'v'
   ensure
      key_in_dictionary:
        has(k)
      value_for_k_is_v:
        value_for(k) = v

The *remove* command must undo the work of *put*, so its postcondition must assert that *has(k)* is false. A common way to assert that something is false is to assert that "not something" is true.

remove (k: KEY)
        -- Remove key 'k' from the dictionary
   ensure
      key_not_in_dictionary:
        not *has(k)*

To complete this part of our story, we need to say that there is no value for a key *k* unless that key is in the dictionary. We need to use *has* in the precondition on *value_for*.

value_for (k: KEY): VALUE
           -- The value associated with key 'k'
    require
        key_in_dictionary:
            has(k)

Now we have said indirectly that *remove(k)* makes *value_for(k)* undefined because we have said:

- *remove* makes *has(k)* false (see the postcondition on *remove*).
- When *has(k)* is false, *value_for(k)* is undefined (see the precondition on *value_for*).

We can help readers of the contract understand this indirect specification by adding a comment to the postcondition of *remove*. The comment states the effect of *remove* on *value_for*.

remove (k: KEY)
           -- Remove key 'k' from the dictionary
    ensure
        key_not_in_dictionary:
            not *has(k)*
        value_for_k_is_undefined:
            -- precondition on *value_for* is false

It is now easier to see that the postcondition on *remove* follows Principle 4 (for each command, write a postcondition that specifies the value of every basic query).

The *initialize* Command We now turn to the last of the commands, the creation command *initialize*. Informally, its postcondition must assert that a newly initialized dictionary is empty, that is, it contains no keys. It would then follow that *value_for(k)* is not defined for any values of *k*.

One way to express the idea that a dictionary contains no keys is to say:

"For all possible *k* of class *KEY*, *has(k)* is false."

We have no simple way to talk about all the possible values that a *KEY* might have. When writing contracts, it is common to want to say "for all objects in this set of objects, such-and-such a property is true." We return to this topic in Chapter 5.

In this case, there is another way to say that a dictionary contains no keys. We can introduce a new query, a *count* of the number of keys currently in a dictionary, and assert that the *count* is zero. Here, then, is *initialize* with a postcondition that asserts that it sets *count* to zero, with a tag to remind readers of the significance of a zero *count*.

initialize
        -- Initialize a dictionary to be empty
    ensure
        dictionary_is_empty:
            count = 0

We now have several tasks to complete.

1. Determine that *count* is a basic query.
2. Decide whether any other queries now become derived queries.
3. Make sure that every command specifies its effect on every basic query.

The new query *count* seems to be a basic query. It cannot be derived from the existing queries *has* and *value_for*. And they cannot be derived from *count*. So, now we have three basic queries. Therefore, we must make sure that every command specifies its effect on all three basic queries.

The *put* Command Revisited When we *put* a new key into a dictionary, we expect the *count* to increase by one. Here is a revised version of the *put* command that defines its effect on all three basic queries.

put (k: KEY; v: VALUE)
      -- Put key 'k' into the dictionary with associated value 'v'
   ensure
     count_increased:
        *count = **old** count + 1*
     key_in_dictionary:
        has(k)
     value_for_k_is_v:
        value_for(k) = v

This contract has two small problems. First, if *put* is called with a key *k* that is already in the dictionary, the *count* of the number of keys does not increase. We address this problem in two ways. In Section 3.5, when we apply principle P5 and look carefully at preconditions, we will constrain clients not to call *put* with a key that is already in the dictionary. Later, we will suggest an exercise in which you explore an alternative version of *put*.

Second, how can we be sure, for example, that adding one key, which by the above postcondition makes *has(k)* true, does not make *has(...)* true for lots of other potential keys as well? The answer is that we assume that there is an extra rule, not stated explicitly and not automatically checked, that says "and nothing else changes." In Chapter 7, we explore how to add explicit frame rules, as these kinds of rules are known.

The *remove* Command Revisited When we *remove* a key from a dictionary, the *count* of the number of keys goes down by one. Here is *remove* with a postcondition that specifies its effect on all three basic queries. Once again, you might be able to spot a problem with this postcondition, a problem that can be fixed by an appropriate precondition.

remove (k: KEY)
      -- Remove key 'k' from the dictionary

ensure

    count_decreased:

        *count = **old** count – 1*

    key_not_in_dictionary:

        not *has(k)*

    value_for_k_is_undefined:

        -- precondition on value_for is false

The *initialize* Command Revisited We have already decided that when we *initialize* a new dictionary, its *count* is zero:

initialize

    -- Initialize a dictionary to be empty

    ensure

    dictionary_is_empty:

        count = 0

To specify the effect of *initialize* on all three basic queries, we need to add that *has(k)* is false for every possible *k*, and that *value_for(k)* is not defined for any *k*.

We solved the problem of how to say that *value_for(k)* is not defined when we were working on *remove*. We solved it by placing a precondition on *value_for* that *has(k)* must be true.

Now we turn our attention to *has(k)*. We want to say in the postcondition of *initialize* that:

    "For all possible keys, *has(k)* is false."

This needs a "forall" that works over all possible keys, and we introduced the *count* query precisely to get around the problem of needing such a "forall," so it appears that we have made no progress.

We are stuck on trying to specify something about *has* in the postcondition on *initialize*. What happens if we turn the problem around? Can we go to the *has* feature and there express the fact that *has(k)* is false after *initialize*?

We have already asserted that *initialize* sets *count* to zero. In the postcondition on *has* we can assert that, if the *count* is zero, the *Result* of *has* must be false.

```
has (k: KEY): BOOLEAN
        -- Does the dictionary contain key 'k'?
    ensure
        consistent_with_count:
            (count = 0) implies (not Result)
```

The logical operator **implies** allows us to write an expression that you can read as saying "**if** the *count* is zero **then** the *Result* is false."

We have now said that:

- A newly initialized dictionary has a *count* of zero (see the postcondition on *initialize*).
- When a dictionary's *count* is zero, the value of *has(k)* is false, no matter what argument *k* it is called with (see the postcondition on *has*).

In other words, we have said that a newly created dictionary returns *false* in reply to the query *has(k)*, and it does so for every possible *k*.

We have also said that:

- In a newly initialized dictionary, *value_for(k)* is undefined for all values of *k* (the precondition on *value_for* requires that *has(k)* is true, yet, as we have just argued, *has(k)* is false for all *k* in a newly initialized dictionary).

We have now achieved our goal of specifying the effect of each command on every query. In doing so, we have already begun to think about preconditions. Now it's time to look at preconditions systematically.

3.5 PRECONDITIONS

The fifth of our principles says this:

> **P**rinciple 5   **For every query and command, decide on a suitable precondition.** Preconditions constrain when clients may call the queries and commands.

We will examine each feature in turn and decide whether it needs a precondition. Sometimes, the decision can only be made if you know the kind of software you are developing. For example, if you are writing a class that is needed in a particular application, and it is needed quickly, you might choose preconditions that make life easier for the implementer. By contrast, if you are writing a class to go into a library of reusable classes, you will want to choose less stringent preconditions to make life easier for client programmers.

In this section, we'll start with some preconditions that make life easier for the implementer and then explore how they could be made less stringent in the Things to Do section.

The *count* and *has* Queries   There is no reason to prevent clients from asking how many keys a dictionary contains or whether it contains a particular key. The *count* and *has* features do not need preconditions.

The *value_for* Query   We have already given *value_for* a precondition to prevent clients from asking for the *value_for* a key that is not in the dictionary. There is no need to add to this precondition.

The *initialize* Command   We must keep a technical point in mind here. The *initialize* command is called to initialize a newly created object, so the precondition on *initialize* cannot say that the object must be in such-and-such a state before *initialize* is called. If the *initialize* routine had arguments, they could be constrained by a precondition, but this *initialize* has no arguments. So, the *initialize* routine must not have a precondition.

The *put* Command   One of the exercises in the Things to Do section asks you to think about redesigning class *DICTIONARY* so that it is protected against being overfilled. Here, we will continue with a simple version, which assumes there is enough memory.

But we might want to place a constraint on clients of *put*. The signature of *put* is this:

put (k: KEY; v: VALUE)
> -- Put key 'k' into the dictionary with associated value 'v'

For a dictionary to work, the keys must all be different. The simplest way to make sure that they are is to place a constraint on clients not to *put* a key into the dictionary if it is already there.

> **require**
>> k_not_already_there:
>>> **not** *has(k)*

This is not the only solution. The Things to Do section invites you to consider an alternative design.

We might want to place another constraint on clients. We might require that *k* does not hold a *Void* reference.

> **require**
>> k_exists:
>>> *k /= Void*

Void is Eiffel's term for the nil pointer, and the operator "/=" is Eiffel's "not equal to." This second constraint is at a different level of abstraction. It is not about the conceptual level at which we can talk about the properties of a look-up table and contrast them with the properties of a stack. It is concerned with a detail of object technology. Some variables can hold references to objects. These references can be *Void*. As designers of class *DICTIONARY*, we need to choose whether a *Void* reference is a possible key. For now, we will decide that a *Void* reference is not allowed as a key, and we'll explore the alternative in the Things to Do section. Also for now, we will allow a *Void* reference for the value associated with a key (you might want to put someone's name in your e-mail address book, and add the e-mail address later).

We call *k /= Void* a physical constraint because it concerns the physical aspects of the underlying technology. We call ***not** has(k)* a logical constraint because it concerns the logical, or conceptual, properties of dictionaries.

The complete contract on *put* contains five assertions.

put (k: KEY; v: VALUE)
        -- Put key 'k' into the dictionary with associated value 'v'
  require
     k_exists:
        k /= Void
     k_not_in_dictionary:
        ***not** has(k)*
  ensure
     count_increased:
        *count = **old** count + 1*
     key_in_dictionary:
        has(k)
     value_for_k_is_v:
        value_for(k) = v

In developing this contract, we have introduced the idea of physical constraints, which are different from logical constraints. A new principle is not really at work here, so we'll start a list of guidelines for those developing contracts, to add to the list of six principles. We'll add more guidelines in later chapters.

> **GUIDELINE 1   Add physical constraints where appropriate.** Typically these will be constraints that variables should not be void.

A small but important detail: Eiffel combines individual clauses in preconditions and postconditions with the logical operator it calls ***and then***, which evaluates its second operand only if the first is true. We must sometimes pay attention to the order of the clauses. For example, if the query *has* cannot accept a *Void* argument, we must arrange that the precondition *k /= Void* is checked before the precondi-ton **not** *has(k)*, by putting that test first.

The *remove* Command If we take *remove* to have its English meaning, you cannot remove a key that is not already in a dictionary. We could decide to place a constraint on clients only to call *remove* with a key that is in the dictionary, like this:

remove (k: KEY)
> -- Remove key 'k' from the dictionary

   require
> key_in_dictionary:
> > *has(k)*

   ensure
> count_decreased:
> > *count =* **old** *count - 1*
> key_not_in_dictionary:
> > **not** *has(k)*
> value_for_k_is_undefined:
> > -- Precondition for *value_for* is false

If we think about *remove* as an operation on a software object, rather than just an English word, we might decide that an attempt to *remove* a key that is not there has no effect, but is perfectly allowable. In other words, we could concentrate on the fact that the significant outcome of *remove* is that *has(k)* false, whether it was true or false before.

Once again, we start with the precondition that is easier to implement and invite you to explore alternatives in the Things to Do section. As always, there is no right answer to a design problem. Design involves choosing between alternatives, based on competing pressures.

When we considered the precondition on *put*, we introduced a physical con-straint, that *k* must not be *Void*. Do we need the same physical constraint here, on *remove*? We can argue as follows. For a given dictionary, the precondition on *put* prevents clients from putting void keys into the dictionary. The precondition on *remove* requires clients to provide a key that is in the dictionary. Therefore a client is already constrained not to call *remove* with a void key. Therefore a precondition on *remove* saying *k/= Void* would not be an additional constraint.

However, somewhere, we must begin to document this interaction between *put* and *remove* and their contracts to help any developer who is thinking of changing something about the class. And an obvious place to do that is in a precondition. Here is the finished contract for *remove*. From a client's point of view, the precondition states that *remove* is not to be called with a void key, or a key that is not in the dictionary. From the point of view of a developer thinking of changing the class, the precondition says "the implementation can assume that *k* is not void and that *k* is already in the dictionary. If you relax either of these constraints, you might need to change the implementation code."

remove (k: KEY)
          -- Remove key 'k' from the dictionary
     require
          key_exists:
               k /= Void
          key_in_dictionary:
               has(k)
     ensure
          count_decreased:
               count = **old** *count – 1*
          key_not_in_dictionary:
               not *has(k)*
          value_for_k_is_undefined:
               -- Precondition for *value_for* is false

Physical Constraints on Queries We have two queries, *has* and *value_for*, that both take a key as an argument. Should they both have the following physical-level precondition?

     require
          key_exists:
               k /= Void

There are arguments for including it and for omitting it. As usual in design, there is no single right answer.

If the dictionary never contains void keys, the query *has(k)*, for instance, will return **false** when *k* is void, so there is no problem in omitting the constraint. And the query *value_for* is constrained by *has(k)*, so that's all right, too.

On the other hand, client programmers might like to be told when they accidentally pass a void key to a dictionary query.

Experienced designers will recognize that we are trying to guess what our client programmers want. The answer to that dilemma is to give them the choice. One of the exercises in the Things to Do section is about making a dictionary that will or will not accept void keys in its queries and commands.

For now, we will remain consistent with earlier decisions and place physical constraints on the queries, too. This makes it easier for us to implement the class.

3.6   INVARIANT

The last of our six principles concerns invariant properties of objects.

> **P**RINCIPLE 6   **Write invariants to define unchanging properties of objects.** Concentrate on properties that help the reader build an appropriate conceptual model of the abstraction the class embodies.

As designers of the class *DICTIONARY*, we know that the *count* of the number of keys can never be negative. We can do two things with this fact. We can argue why it is so, and we can record it.

The argument is quite subtle and goes like this. There is only one creation routine, *initialize*, and it sets *count* to zero. There are two other commands. One, *put*, increases the *count*. If *put* is called when the *count* is non-negative, it leaves it non-negative. The other command, *remove*, reduces the *count*. But *remove* has a precondition that the key to be removed is in the dictionary, expressed in the assertion *has(k)*. The postcondition on *has* ensures that it will return false when the *count* is zero. Therefore, it is impossible to call *remove* unless the *count* is positive. The lowest positive value of *count* is one. A call to *remove* when the *count* is one will reduce the *count* to zero. Therefore, it is impossible for the *count* to go negative.

To record this fact, we add an invariant to the class.

invariant
    count_never_negative:
        count >= 0

Now, of course, we can have it checked at runtime during development and testing.

3.7 A COMPLETE, CONTRACT-LEVEL VIEW OF DICTIONARY

Here, in one place, are all the features of class DICTIONARY and their contracts. By now, you should find reading such client-oriented views quite straightforward.

indexing
    description: "Dictionaries hold keys. Each key has an associated value."

class interface
    DICTIONARY [KEY, VALUE]

creation
    initialize

feature -- 1. Basic queries

    count: INTEGER
        -- The number of keys in the dictionary

has (k: KEY): BOOLEAN
> -- Does the dictionary contain key 'k'?

require
> key_exists: *k /= void*

ensure
> consistent_with_count: *(count = 0)* **implies** (**not** *Result)*

value_for (k: KEY): VALUE
> -- The value associated with key 'k'

require
> key_exists: *k /= void*
> key_in_dictionary: *has (k)*

feature -- 2. Creation commands

initialize
> -- Initialize a dictionary to be empty

ensure
> dictionary_is_empty: *count = 0*

feature -- 3. Other commands

put (k: KEY; v: VALUE)
> -- Put key 'k' into the dictionary with associated value 'v'

require
> key_exists: *k /= void*
> key_not_in_dictionary: **not** *has (k)*

ensure
> count_increased: *count =* **old** *count + 1*
> key_in_dictionary: *has (k)*
> value_for_k_is_v: *value_for (k) = v*

remove (k: KEY)
> -- Remove key 'k' from the dictionary

require
> key_exists: *k /= void*
> key_in_dictionary: *has (k)*

ensure
>   count_decreased: *count* = **old** *count* − *1*
>   key_not_in_dictionary: **not** *has (k)*
>   value_for_k_is_undefined:
>   -- Precondition on *value_for* is false for argument 'k'

invariant
>   count_never_negative: *count* >= *0*

end -- class DICTIONARY

3.8 SUMMARY

In this chapter we have developed comprehensive contracts on the features of class DICTIONARY:

value_for(k)
initialize
put(k, v)
remove(k)

To do so, we introduced further features:

count
has(k)

To show that we had followed the six principles (particularly P3 and P4 relating to postconditions), we constructed arguments about how the features and their contracts work together.

The argument that *initialize* defines the query *value_for(k)* looks straightforward in hindsight.

- *initialize* sets *count* to zero (see the postcondition on *initialize*).
- When *count* is zero, *has(k)* is false for every *k* (see the postcondition on *has*).
- When *has(k)* is false, *value_for(k)* is undefined (see the precondition on *value_for*).

Developing the argument and designing the features and their contracts to support it were not straightforward activities. However, the final design contains ideas that you can use elsewhere (notably, the idea of a *has* query and its relationship to *count*).

And the final design presents the following conceptual model of a dictionary. At any one moment, a dictionary either *has* or does not have a particular key. You can *count* the keys a dictionary *has*. When a dictionary *has* a particular key, you can ask for the *value_for* that key.

We introduced the first of several guidelines to go with our six principles. This first one suggests explicitly adding physical constraints (for example, to ban void arguments to features).

In these first three chapters, we have developed contracts that specify how commands change the state of an object, as seen through its queries. For example, the postcondition on the *put* feature in class DICTIONARY asserts that the dictionary now has the key just *put*. It does not assert that all the keys that were already in the dictionary are still there, and they still have the same associated values. You can think of the contracts we have developed so far as "change specs." In Chapter 7, we explore "no change specs," known as frame rules.

3.9 THINGS TO DO

From the book's Web site, you can download a simple implementation of class DICTIONARY, with a small demo program to try it out. If you do not have an Eiffel compiler, develop a simple implementation of our dictionary class in a language for which you have support for contracts.

1. Add the following features to the class DICTIONARY, taking care to follow the six principles when formulating their contracts:

    *   *is_empty : BOOLEAN* -- does the dictionary contain no keys?
    *   *replace(k : KEY ; v : VALUE)* -- replace the value for 'k' by 'v'

2. Remove various parts of the precondition on the *put* feature (the postcondition might change, too, and it might be harder to implement):

   • Remove the physical precondition that disallows void keys. What changes do you have to make to the postcondition? To the implementation? (Hint: You'll have to introduce extra checks before using variables of type *KEY* when void values are allowed.)

   • Remove the logical precondition that the key is not already in the dictionary. Again, what changes do you need to make to the postcondition? Consider two variations of what *put* means when called with an existing key: it has no effect, or it behaves as a *replace* command. Implement your variations, and give them contracts.

3. [Harder] Provide a way to switch "void keys allowed" on or off in the *initialize* command. Add a suitable query for clients to determine the state of the switch. Rewrite all contracts to take account of the state of the switch.

4. Add a local performance enhancement to your implementation. Always cache the result of *has(k)* so that you speed up the evaluation of *value_for(k)* whenever a client performs a call to *has* immediately followed by a call to *value_for*. What impact does the change have on the contract view of the class?

5. [Harder] The *put* routine remembers a value *v* for a key *k*. The client that called *put* shares a reference to *v* with the dictionary and could change *v* while it is in the dictionary. What if the *put* routine remembers a **copy** of the value, instead? Implement such a routine (call it *put_copy_of_value*), and write a contract for it.

6. [Harder] We have been making an assumption, without stating it, that no routine changes its arguments. Can you use contracts to say, for instance, that putting a key into a dictionary does not change the key?

Building Support for Contracts— Immutable Lists

4.1 ABOUT THIS CHAPTER

This chapter develops a special kind of list class—immutable lists—to be used to support contracts in other classes. In doing so, it

- Defines the objects of the list class as immutable—once they have been constructed, they cannot be changed.
- Explains that the contracts on the list class involve recursion.
- Mentions turning contract-checking on and off because recursive contracts can be expensive to check.

In Chapter 5, we use the list class developed here to write the contract on a queue class, and we discuss turning contract-checking on and off more fully.

4.2 SUPPORT FOR LINEAR STRUCTURES

In Chapter 2, we looked at the STACK class, which is one example of a linear structure. In Chapter 5 we will look at another example, QUEUE.

In Chapter 2, we introduced this query into the STACK class:

item_at(i : INTEGER) : G

We introduced it in order to support contracts on the more usual stack features, such as *put* and *remove*. In this chapter, we are going to go a step further and build a special list class to make it easier to support contracts on regular features of linear-structure classes, such as stacks and queues. We ask you to trust that the list class we build will be useful. That way, we won't have to mix two kinds of explanations—explanations of what we are building (in this chapter) and explanations of how and why it will be useful (which come in Chapter 5).

4.3 CONTRACTS INVOLVE EXPRESSIONS

A typical contract on a feature in a class looks like this one, taken from the DICTIONARY class:

put(k : KEY; v : VALUE) is
        -- Put key 'k' into the dictionary with associated value 'v'
  require
    key_exists:
      k /= Void
    key_not_in_dictionary:
      not has(k)
  ensure
    count_increased:
      *count = **old** count + 1*
    key_in_dictionary:
      has(k)
    value_for_k_is_v:
      value_for(k) = v
  end

The assertions in the various clauses in the precondition and the postcondition are all expressions. In other words, they have a value (a Boolean value, to be precise). They are not statements. They do not bring about changes.

Certainly, assertions in postconditions can describe changes, using the **old** keyword. But asserting, for example, that

count = **old** *count* + 1*

involves only an expression (in this case, a Boolean test that two values are equal). There must be a statement elsewhere, in the body of the *put* routine, that has the effect of changing the value of the *count*.

Because assertions are expressions, we are going to build a list class that is especially designed for use in expressions. Once an object of this list class has been created and initialized, it will be impossible to change its value. It will be possible to build new lists based on existing lists, using queries within expressions, but there will be no commands for changing an existing list. Objects that are unchangeable once constructed are called *immutable objects*. The next section describes the class of immutable list objects that we will develop.

4.4 IMMUTABLE LISTS

Here is a way to visualize a list of numbers:

[5, 2, 7, 1]

This particular list contains the numbers 5, 2, 7, and 1, in that order.

We can think of this list as having two parts: its first item, called its *head*, and the list of all the other items, called its *tail*. Here is the original list broken into its two parts:

head = 5
tail = [2, 7, 1]

A new list can be built from an existing list, with the items in the original list preceded by a new head. For example, the list [2, 7, 1] preceded by the item 8 yields the new list [8, 2, 7, 1]. We insist that *preceded_by* returns a result, which will be a new, longer list. It will *not* modify the target object. Therefore, *preceded_by* is a query, not a command.

To get the list [2, 7, 1], you begin with a new, empty list, and use *preceded_by* three times to build the list [2], then the list [2, 7], and finally the list [2, 7, 1]. Don't worry about whether this all takes too long at runtime. We'll use *preceded_by* when testing our code, but we'll turn assertion-checking down or even off when we release production code.

So far, we have mentioned three queries on lists: *head, tail,* and *preceded_by.* We will find it useful to have an *is_empty* query to tell us if a list is empty, a *count* query to tell us how many items a list contains, and an *is_equal* query to tell us if two lists hold the same items.

In addition, we introduce an *items(i)* query to look at an arbitrary item of a list, and a *sublist* query for extracting an arbitrary sublist from an existing list.

The UML class diagram in Figure 4.1 summarizes the design so far. The class itself is called IMMUTABLE_LIST and is generic in the types of items it can hold. The various features have been categorized into basic queries, derived queries, and commands. It might not be obvious yet how the categorization was arrived at, but this should become clearer when we write contracts on the features. Observe that the only command is the creation command *initialize.* Observe also that three of the queries deliver newly created lists. Once you have created a new list from an existing one (for instance, by extracting a *sublist*), this new list cannot be changed.

4.5 A CONTRACT FOR IMMUTABLE LISTS

In this section, we develop contracts for the features of the class of immutable lists: its basic queries, its creation command, and its derived queries.

If you are anxious to see how we use immutable lists before diving into the details of how to specify them, you could skip now to Chapter 5, and return here later.

4.5.1 THE BASIC QUERIES

The basic queries on immutable lists are *head, tail,* and *is_empty.* The *head* and *tail* queries make no sense on empty lists, so they have preconditions.

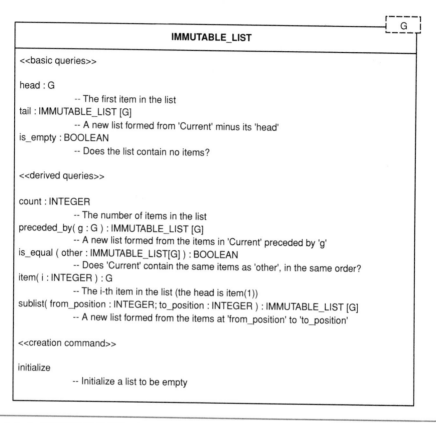

Figure 4.1 An IMMUTABLE_LIST class

head: G
>   -- The first item in the list
>   ***require***
>   not_empty: ***not*** *is_empty*

tail: IMMUTABLE_LIST [G]
>   -- A new list formed from 'Current' minus its 'head'
>   ***require***
>   not_empty: ***not*** *is_empty*

As usual, the basic queries do not have postconditions. Other features have post-conditions that define the values of these basic queries.

4.5.2 THE CREATION COMMAND

The creation command *initialize* takes no arguments, so it cannot have a precondition. Its postcondition asserts that a newly initialized list is empty.

initialize
        -- Initialize a list to be empty
    ensure
        empty: *is_empty*

Because *initialize* ensures that the list *is_empty*, it ensures that neither *head* nor *tail* is a valid query. Therefore, *initialize* defines all three basic queries:

is_empty	value is true	-- see postcondition on make
head	no valid value	-- see precondition on head
tail	no valid value	-- see precondition on tail

4.5.3 THE DERIVED QUERY *COUNT*

The *count* query has the following syntax:

count : INTEGER
        -- The number of items in the list

The postcondition is defined recursively in two parts. For an empty list, the *count* of the number of items is zero. For a nonempty list, the number of items in the whole list is one more than in its *tail.*

    ensure
            is_empty_means_count_is_zero:
                is_empty **implies** *(Result = 0)*
            else_count_is_one_greater_than_count_of_tail:
                *(**not** is_empty)* **implies** *(Result = 1 + tail.count)*

4.5.4 THE DERIVED QUERY *PRECEDED_BY*

The *preceded_by* query has the following syntax:

preceded_by (g:G) : IMMUTABLE_LIST [G]
> -- A new list formed from Current with 'g' added at the head

It must ensure that the result list has *g* as its head, and the receiving list, which we call *Current*, as its tail. It also ensures that the resulting list is not empty.

> **ensure**
>> not_empty: **not** *Result.is_empty*
>> head_is_g: *Result.head* = *g*
>> tail_is_original_list: *Result.tail.is_equal(Current)*

4.5.5 THE DERIVED QUERY *ITEM*

The *item(i)* query returns the i-th item in a list, where *item(1)* is the first, or head, item.

item (i: INTEGER): G
> -- The i-th item in the list (the head is item(1))

It makes no sense to ask for the i-th item unless *i* is between 1 and the *count* of the number of items in the list, so *item* has this precondition:

> *require*
>> i_large_enough: $i >= 1$
>> i_small_enough: $i <= count$

The postcondition is defined recursively and is based on observing that the i-th item of a list is the $(i-1)$-th item of the list's tail, as in the example in Figure 4.2. The postcondition can thus be written as:

> *ensure*
>> base_and_recursive_cases:
>>> $(i = 1$ **and** $Result = head)$
>> *or else*
>>> $Result = tail.item(i - 1)$

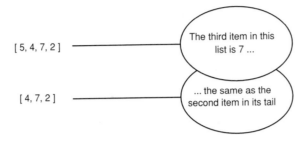

Figure 4.2 A list's i-th item is its tail's (i−1)-th item

(A detail: The use of "or else" makes sure that we don't try to extract the 0-th item from a list of length 1. The operator "or else" evaluates its second operand only if the first is false. We could instead have written two clauses that use ***implies***, as we did in the postcondition of *count*.)

We can try evaluating the postcondition on the list [5, 4, 7, 2], with i = 3. The postcondition tells us that

[5, 4, 7, 2].item(3) =	
[4, 7, 2].item(2) =	-- i.e., item(i − 1) of tail
[7, 2].item(1) =	-- again, item(i − 1) of tail
7	-- this time i = 1 so the result is the head of the list

Here is the complete contract for the *item_at* query.

item (i: INTEGER): G
        -- The i-th item in the list (the head is item_at(1))
    require
        i_large_enough: *i >= 1;*
        i_small_enough: *i <= count*
    ensure
        base_and_recursive_cases:
                (i = 1 ***and*** Result = head)
           or else
                Result = tail.item_at(i − 1)

4.5.6 THE DERIVED QUERY IS_EQUAL

Having seen how we defined the postcondition of *item*, you will not be surprised that the postcondition of *is_equal* also uses recursion over the tail of a list. This time, we present the whole contract and follow it with some explanation.

is_equal (other: IMMUTABLE_LIST [G]): BOOLEAN
        -- Does 'Current' contain the same items as
        -- 'other', in the same order?
require
     other_exists:
          other /= Void
ensure
     same_contents:
          *Result = (is_empty **and** other.is_empty)*
       or else
          (*((**not** is_empty) **and** (**not** other.is_empty))*
        and then
          *(head = other.head **and** tail.is_equal (other.tail)))*

The precondition precludes testing the equality of two lists when one list does not actually exist. The postcondition says that

two lists are equal if, and only if,
    they are both empty
  or
      neither is empty
  and
      their heads are equal **and** their tails are equal

This example shows how *is_equal* arrives recursively at a value of *true*. The example evaluates whether the list [4, 6, 2] is equal to the list [4, 6, 2].

[4, 6, 2].is_equal([4, 6, 2]) =
(4 = 4) and [6, 2].is_equal([6, 2]) =   -- by the last line of the postcondition
true and [6, 2].is_equal([6, 2]) =   -- by the properties of numbers

[6, 2].is_equal([6, 2]) =   -- by the properties of *and*
(6 = 6) and [2].is_equal([2]) =   -- by the last line of the postcondition
true and [2].is_equal([2]) =   -- by the properties of numbers
[2].is_equal([2]) =   -- by the properties of *and*
(2 = 2) and [ ].is_equal([ ]) =   -- by the last line of the postcondition
true and [ ].is_equal([ ]) =   -- by the properties of numbers
[ ].is_equal([ ]) =   -- by the properties of *and*
true   -- by the first line of the postcondition

The last step gives the result *true* because both the receiving object (i.e., *Current*) and the *other* object are empty lists.

This next example shows how *is_equal* arrives at a result of *false*. The example evaluates whether the list [4, 6, 2] is equal to the list [4, 7, 2].

[4, 6, 2].is_equal([4, 7, 2]) =
(4 = 4) and [6, 2].is_equal([7, 2]) =   -- by the last line of the postcondition
true and [6, 2].is_equal([7, 2]) =   -- by the properties of numbers
[6, 2].is_equal([7, 2]) =   -- by the properties of *and*
(6 = 7) and [2].is_equal([2]) =   -- by the last line of the postcondition
false and [2].is_equal([2]) =   -- by the properties of numbers
false   -- by the properties of *and*

The final example shows how *is_equal* arrives at a result of *false* because the lists are of unequal lengths, by evaluating whether the list [4, 6, 2] is equal to the list [4, 6].

[4, 6, 2].is_equal([4, 6]) =
(4 = 4) and [6, 2].is_equal([6]) =   -- by the last line of the postcondition
true and [6, 2].is_equal([6]) =   -- by the properties of numbers
[6, 2].is_equal([6]) =   -- by the properties of *and*
(6 = 6) and [2].is_equal([ ]) =   -- by the last line of the postcondition
true and [2].is_equal([ ]) =   -- by the properties of numbers
[2].is_equal([ ]) =   -- by the properties of *and*
false   -- because the *Current* list *is_empty* but
                                               -- the *other* is not.

4.5.7 THE DERIVED QUERY *SUBLIST*

The *sublist* query extracts a sublist of *Current* between a from position and a to position, inclusive, returning an immutable list.

sublist(from_position : INTEGER; to_position : INTEGER)
$\qquad\qquad\qquad\qquad\qquad\qquad\qquad$ *: IMMUTABLE_LIST [G]*
$\qquad\qquad$ -- A new list formed from the items
$\qquad\qquad$ -- at 'from_position' through 'to_position'

(A tiny detail: We cannot use *from* as a parameter name because it is a reserved word in Eiffel that appears in *loop* statements.)

Our first version of the precondition states that the *from_position* must be at least one, and the *to_position* must lie between the *from_position* and the *count* of the number of items in the list.

> **require**
> $\qquad$ from_position_large_enough: *from_position >= 1*
> $\qquad$ from_position_small_enough: *from_position <= to_position*
> $\qquad$ to_position_small_enough: *to_position <= count*

For example, this precondition allows us to call *sublist* to extract items 2 through 4 of the list [1, 2, 3, 4, 5]. It even allows us to extract a sublist of length 1. For example, we can call *sublist* to extract items 2 through 2 of the list [1, 2, 3, 4, 5]. The result will be the list [2].

But what if we want to extract smaller and smaller sublists from [1, 2, 3, 4, 5] until we have extracted an empty sublist? With our current precondition, there is no way to extract a zero-sized sublist.

A call in which the *from_position* is exactly the same as the *to_position* extracts a sublist of size one. Let us define that a call in which the *from_position* is one greater than the *to_position* extracts a sublist of size zero. In other words, when *from_position = to_position + 1*, we want a zero-sized result. For example, the sublist from 3 through 2 of [1, 2, 3, 4, 5] is the empty list [ ]. In the following table, the *from_position* is increased until the *Result* list is empty:

Current	from_position	to_position	Result
[1, 2, 3, 4, 5]	2	4	[2, 3, 4]
[1, 2, 3, 4, 5]	3	4	[3, 4]
[1, 2, 3, 4, 5]	4	4	[4]
[1, 2, 3, 4, 5]	5	4	[ ]

Our adjusted precondition has a slightly different second clause:

require
    from_position_large_enough: *from_position >= 1*
    from_position_small_enough: *from_position <= to_position + 1*
    to_position_small_enough: *to_position <= count*

The postcondition defines that the *Result.is_empty* whenever the *from_position* is greater than the *to_position* (i.e., when we have created an empty *Result* sublist):

ensure
    is_empty_consistent_with_from_and_to_position:
        Result.is_empty = (from_position > to_position)

The postcondition also defines that the items in the result are those in the relevant portion of the original list. This part of the postcondition has two clauses. The first defines that the *head* of the *Result* is the *item(from_position)* in *Current* (this clause applies only when the *Result* list is not empty).

Result_head_is_at_from_position_in_Current:
    (from_position <= to_position) implies
        (Result.head = item(from_position))

The second clause defines that the *tail* of the *Result* is equal to the *sublist* of *Current* to be found at positions *from_position+1* through *to_position* (this clause applies only when the *Result* list is long enough to have a tail).

Result_tail_is_correct_sublist_within_Current:
   (from_position <= to_position) implies
      (Result.tail.is_equal(sublist(from_position + 1, to_position)))

4.6 SUMMARY

In this chapter, we have developed a contract for a class of immutable lists. We used recursion in the postconditions of several features.

We designed the class to have features that will help us write contracts on classes that handle linear structures, such as stacks and queues. The design will make more sense when we use immutable lists in the contract on a simple queue class in Chapter 5.

4.7 THINGS TO DO

1. In the postcondition of *count,* we used two clauses each using the ***implies*** keyword. In the postcondition of *item_at,* we used an ***or else*** to achieve a similar effect. Rewrite *count* using ***or else*** and rewrite *item* using ***implies***. Do you draw any conclusions?

2. Add a new feature to the immutable list class, such as *reverse* a list, and define a contract for it.

3. Compare execution times of a test program for different levels of assertion-checking (e.g., full checking, precondition-only checking, and no checking at all).

4. [Harder] A contract can contain calls to features that themselves have contracts. Eiffel does not check assertions in features called during an assertion check. Devise an experiment to demonstrate that this is so. Devise an example of a contract where, if Eiffel was not defined this way, there would be an assertion failure even though the code and contracts contained no bugs.

5. [For those who know something of the theory of recursion] Prove that the recursive contracts we have defined in this chapter are well grounded in the basic queries.

Applying the Six Principles to QUEUE

5.1 ABOUT THIS CHAPTER

This chapter applies the six principles introduced in Chapter 2 to the class QUEUE. In doing so, it

- Assumes that the contracts on QUEUE are based on a query that returns a list containing all the items in a queue. This query uses the list class developed in Chapter 4.
- Shows how to place a postcondition on an attribute, using the class invariant.
- Discusses the benefits of making preconditions cheap to evaluate.

5.2 QUEUES

Figure 5.1 shows the key features of a class based on a simple concept of queues.

A queue can hold items of some type G. You can *initialize* a newly created queue to have a certain *capacity* (to keep things simple, we won't provide a way to change the capacity). When you *put* an item into a queue, it goes at the tail. You can ask for the item at the *head* of the queue, and you can *remove* this head item from the queue.

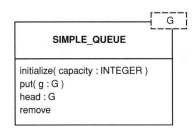

Figure 5.1 The key features of a SIMPLE_QUEUE class

In the following sections, we develop contracts for these features. In doing so, we introduce further features: a simple query *count* that tells us how many items a queue holds, a query *items* that returns a list of the items currently in the queue, and a query *capacity* that tells us how many items a queue can hold.

5.3 A Contract for the *REMOVE* Feature

In this section, we develop a contract for the *remove* feature. To support this contract, we introduce several additional queries, including a simple query, *count*, that tells us how many items a queue holds, and a more complicated query, *items*, that tells us all the items in a queue.

The queries we introduce in order to write the contract for *remove* are a good basis for writing the contracts for the other features, which is why we start with *remove*.

Here is the signature of the *remove* feature.

remove
        -- Remove the item at the head

If the queue is empty, there is no item to remove, so we begin by writing a pre-condition on *remove* to say that the queue must have something in it. (There is an alternative, which is to design *remove* so that it does nothing if the queue is empty. A discussion of which design is better is really a discussion about class design, not about contracts.)

To be able to say that the queue is empty, we could introduce a Boolean query *is_empty*, or an integer-valued query *count* that tells us how many items a queue holds. As well as supporting the precondition on *remove*, a feature *count* will show up in the postcondition. One of the effects of *remove* is to reduce the *count* by one. So, we begin by introducing *count* and later consider adding an *is_empty* query.

Here is what we have so far. We have an additional feature, *count*, and it is used in the precondition and the postcondition of *remove*.

count : INTEGER
    -- The number of items in the queue

remove
    -- Remove the item at the head
  require
    not_empty:
      count > 0
  ensure
    count_decreased:
      *count = **old** count − 1*

Is it enough to say, in the postcondition of *remove*, that the *count* is reduced by one? The answer is no, it is not. We also need to say that the item that is now at the head of the queue is the one that used to be second in the queue, and the item that is now second in the queue used to be third in the queue, and so on. In general, the item now at position i in the queue used to be at position i + 1.

Informally we can write an assertion to capture this.

    -- The items that are now in positions 1 through *count*
    -- used to be in positions 2 through **old** *count*

By introducing a suitable query, we can talk about the "items in positions *m* through *n*." We introduce an *items* query:

items : IMMUTABLE_LIST[G]
        -- A new list containing the items in
        -- the queue, in queue order

The IMMUTABLE_LIST class was introduced in Chapter 4. The *items* query returns a newly created immutable list containing all the items in the queue.

If you were to add "a", "b", and "c" to an empty queue of string objects, the *items* query would return a list that could be visualized like this:

["a", "b", "c"]

If you were to remove the string at the head of the queue, the list of the queue's *items* would look like this:

["b", "c"]

The string "b" used to be in position 2 in the queue, and now it is in position 1 (the head). As a final example, if you were now to add the string "d" to the queue, it would go at the tail, and the *items* in the queue would look like this:

["b", "c", "d"]

At each step, *items* is a new list object. It is always exactly the right size for the job. The *items* object is not the actual data structure that holds the elements in the queue in the implementation, but is calculated from it.

We are going to make use of the *tail* feature of the IMMUTABLE_LIST class. This returns a new list that is a copy of the original list without its head item.

tail : IMMUTABLE_LIST[G]
        -- A new list formed from 'Current' minus its 'head'

We can use Eiffel's **old** operator together with the *tail* feature to say that the items in a queue after a *remove* are those that used to be in positions 2 through the end of the queue. Here it is as an Eiffel assertion.

*items.is_equal (***old** *items.tail)*

Putting all the pieces of the *remove* feature together (including a lengthier header comment), we get this finished version:

remove
            -- Remove the item at the head
            -- Shift the item that used to be in position 2 to
            -- the head of the queue
            -- Shift the item that used to be in position 3 to
            -- position 2
            -- And so on
      require
            not_empty:
                  count > 0
      ensure
            number_of_items_decreased:
                  *count = ***old** *count – 1*
            items_shifted:
                  *items.is_equal (***old** *items.tail)*

There is some redundancy in the two postcondition clauses. If *items* is now equal to what was the tail of *items,* there must be one fewer item in the queue. Therefore, the *count* must be one fewer. We'll shortly make *count* a derived query and later invite you to rewrite the contract.

As an example, suppose that the QUEUE class is implemented using an array to hold the items in a queue. Imagine a particular queue object, initialized to hold up to three items and filled with three strings, "a", "b", and "c" (see Figure 5.2).

The *items* query applied to this queue object returns the immutable list ["a", "b", "c"]. After a call to *remove* a string from the queue, the array that represents the

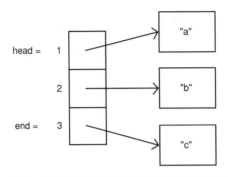

Figure 5.2 A queue holding "a," "b", and "c"

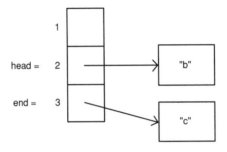

Figure 5.3 The queue after a call to *remove*

queue might be as shown in Figure 5.3 (imagine, for example, that the array is being treated as a circular structure to give an efficient implementation).

The array is still of length three, but now holds only two strings. The *items* query applied to this queue returns ["b", "c"], a new list, of length two. And this list of two items is equal to the tail of the earlier list of three items.

5.4 MAKING *COUNT* A DERIVED FEATURE

In this section, we explore two aspects of the *count* feature of class QUEUE. First, we show how it can be made into a derived feature by defining it to equal the length of the *items* list. This introduces a technique for writing postconditions on attributes (we make use of the class invariant). Second, we explore getting rid of *count* entirely and always working with the length of *items*. We conclude that *count* has a role to play, for performance reasons. In a final subsection, we add to our list of guidelines to summarize the topics covered.

The class IMMUTABLE_LIST provides a *count* feature. If *items* is a list, *items.count* is the number of items in the list. In principle, the *count* feature in class QUEUE can be specified in terms of the *count* feature of class IMMUTABLE_LIST, like this:

count : INTEGER
        -- The number of items in the queue
    ensure
        consistent_with_items:
            Result = items.count

It is a limitation in Eiffel that you cannot write a contract directly on an attribute, only on a function or a procedure. However, for postconditions on attributes, the class invariant can be used to overcome this limitation. What the preceding post-condition on *count* says is that the value of the *count* query is always equal to the value of the *items.count* query. We can express this fact in an invariant, as follows:

invariant
    count_consistent_with_items:
        count = items.count

To help our readers, we can declare *count* like this:

feature
    count : INTEGER
            -- The number of items in the queue
        -- ensure
        --   Result = items.count
        --   (See invariant.)

As an alternative approach, we could add a *count* function, rename the underlying attribute, and make the attribute private. Then we could place the postcondition on this *count* function directly.

We now turn to the second issue concerning *count*. If its value is always equal to *items.count*, why do we need it at all? For instance, we could rewrite the precondition on *remove* to use *items.count* directly, like this:

remove
        -- Remove the oldest item from the queue
    require
       not_empty:
          items.count > 0

This version of the precondition is much more expensive to evaluate than the version that used the *count* attribute. This is because evaluating *items.count* involves constructing the immutable list *items*, which is expensive to do.

Of course, if we retain the attribute *count*, the check we placed in the invariant—that it always equals *items.count*—is just as expensive to evaluate. So where is the benefit in retaining *count*?

During the development of a class, it is usually best to work with the highest possible level of assertion-checking, in which preconditions, postconditions, and invariants are all checked on every appropriate occasion. Once a class has passed its inspections and tests, it is common practice to reduce the level of assertion-checking to precondition-checking only because then the code runs more quickly and development of the class's clients proceeds more rapidly.

The rationale is this. Invariants and postconditions catch bugs in the code that is written as a class is being developed and tested. Preconditions catch bugs in the clients of the class. When a class is ready for general use by clients, we want to protect it from calls that do not respect preconditions. We do not need to slow clients down by repeating the full assertion-checking carried out during the class's development (of course, if during the development of a client, it appears that there is a bug in the original class, we can turn full assertion-checking back on).

So, imagine that we are going to leave precondition-checking on in class QUEUE to help those writing clients of QUEUE, but we will turn off invariant and postcondition checking because they slow execution too much. We will not be helping programmers developing clients of class QUEUE if checking preconditions is very slow. Therefore, we will keep the *count* attribute precisely because it makes evaluating the precondition on *remove* very quick. But to make sure that *count* delivers the correct result, we will develop, inspect, and test the class QUEUE with an invariant clause that checks that *count* always equals *items.count.*

We have arrived at two more pieces of advice for those writing contracts, which we summarize as guidelines.

> **G**UIDELINE 2   **Make sure that queries used in preconditions are cheap to calculate.** If necessary, add cheap-to-calculate derived queries whose postconditions verify them against more expensive queries.

> **G**UIDELINE 3   **Constrain attributes using an invariant.** When a derived query is implemented as an attribute, it can be constrained to be consistent with other queries by an assertion in the class's invariant section.

5.5   A CONTRACT FOR THE *INITIALIZE* FEATURE

The *initialize* command can be used to initialize a newly created queue object or to reinitialize an existing queue object. It takes a single argument, called *a_capacity*, which controls how many items the queue object can hold (remember, to keep things simple, we will not change a queue's *capacity*). Here is an informal version of the contract for *initialize*.

initialize(a_capacity : INTEGER)
>> -- Initialize *Current* to be empty but
>> -- capable of holding up to *a_capacity* items
> **require**
>> -- *a_capacity* must be at least one
> **ensure**
>> -- Capacity of queue has been set to *a_capacity;*
>> -- Queue is empty (i.e., contains no items)

The precondition prevents a client asking for a queue with a capacity of, for example, minus 3. To allow us to express this precondition formally, we must add a query to the class that tells us its capacity. We introduce the following query:

capacity : INTEGER
>> -- How many items *Current* can hold

This query can be used in the postcondition of *initialize* to assert that the parameter *a_capacity* has been remembered. Here is the declaration of *initialize* again, this time with a formal contract.

initialize(a_capacity : INTEGER)
>> -- Initialize *Current* to be empty but
>> -- capable of holding up to *a_capacity* items
> **require**
>> a_capacity_positive:
>>> *a_capacity >= 1*
> **ensure**
>> capacity_set:
>>> *capacity = a_capacity*
>> empty:
>>> *count = 0*

The second part of the postcondition uses the *count* feature to assert that there are no items in a just-initialized queue.

5.6   A CONTRACT FOR THE *HEAD* FEATURE

Informally, the *head* feature is declared as follows:

head : G
        -- The item at the head
    require
        -- Queue is not empty
    ensure
        -- Result is the first item in the queue

The postcondition talks about the first item in the queue. The *items* query returns a list containing all the items in the queue. Although we have not said so explicitly yet, we have already decided that the head of this list tells us the first item in the queue. (We made this decision when we chose how to specify *remove.*) Therefore, we can define the *head* of a queue in terms of the *head* of the list of *items* it contains.

The precondition talks about a queue not being empty. A queue is not empty whenever the *count* of the number of items is at least one.

We can formalize the contract on *head,* as follows:

head : G
        -- The item at the head
    require
        not_empty:
            count >= 1
    ensure
        consistent_with_items:
            Result = items.head

The *head* query is formally defined in terms of existing queries, so *head* is a derived query.

Once again, we have a feature whose postcondition is expensive to evaluate (because it involves calculating the *items* list) but whose precondition is cheap to evaluate (it only involves the *count* attribute).

5.7 A Contract for the *put* Feature

The *items* and *capacity* features introduced in previous sections can be used to specify how *put* behaves. Here is the declaration of *put* with a contract.

put(g : G)
        -- Add *g* to the tail of the queue
  require
    not_full:
      count < capacity
  ensure
    number_of_items_increased:
      count = **old** *count + 1*
    g_at_tail:
      items.item(count) = g

The second part of the postcondition uses an expression of the form *items.item(i)* to talk about the i-th item in the *items* list. In this case, *i* is *count*. More specifically, it is the new value of *count*, which is one more than the old value.

As always, we are assuming that, if we don't assert that something changes, then it doesn't. We take up this issue seriously in Chapter 7 when we look at frame rules.

5.8 More Derived Queries

The *count* query introduced earlier can be used to test whether a queue object is empty or full. We can introduce shorthands for these special cases, *is_empty* and *is_full*, both of which are derived queries.

is_empty: BOOLEAN
      -- Does the queue contain no items?
  ensure
      consistent_with_items_count:
         Result = (items.count = 0)

is_full: BOOLEAN
      -- Does the queue have no room for another item?
  ensure
      consistent_with_items_count_and_capacity:
         Result = (items.count = capacity)

5.9   SUMMARY

We now have contracts on the four features introduced in Section 5.2: *initialize*, *put*, *head*, and *remove*. To be able to write the contracts, we introduced two further features, *items* and *capacity*, both of which are primitive queries. We noted that the *head* query is a derived query. We also introduced a *count* query on a queue and made it into a derived query. A clause in the invariant defines that it is derived from the size of the *items* list, as given by *items.count*. Finally, we introduced derived queries *is_empty* and *is_full*.

The class diagram in Figure 5.4 summarizes the features and their categories.

If you are not used to writing contracts on classes, you might have been startled by the introduction of the *items* query. Doesn't it break encapsulation? Aren't we exposing internal details of the class? We asked a similar question when developing the contract for class STACK in Chapter 2, and again the answer is a firm no. If you have access to the *head* and *remove* features, you can find out for yourself what all the items in a queue are. (For a simple way to do this, imagine sitting in a loop calling *head* then *remove* until the queue is empty. Along the way, you will have looked at every item in the queue.)

Providing a list that tells you all the items at one go is not telling you anything you cannot already find out. Of course, if we gave you a way to *insert* an element

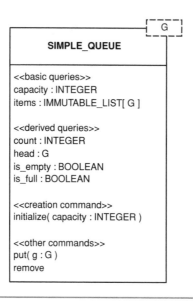

Figure 5.4 The redesigned queue class

at an arbitrary point, we would be offering you a class that did not implement the popular idea of a first-in, first-out queue, and that would be quite a different matter.

5.10 THINGS TO DO

You can download a prototype Eiffel queue class from the book's Web site, together with the IMMUTABLE_LIST class used in its contract. If you are working in another language, write your own implementation of a queue class to work with. (If you are working with an assertion language that provides a "forall" operator, you probably won't need an IMMUTABLE_LIST class.)

1. Play with the classes. Put bugs into the bodies of routines, and see if the contracts catch them. Put bugs into the assertions in the contracts and see what happens.

2. Add some features to the QUEUE class, and give them contracts. Implement and test them. Here are some suggestions:

   - *clear*—remove all items, but leave *capacity* the same.
   - *requeue_head*—remove the head item and put it back at the tail of the queue.
   - *is_equal*—test whether two queues hold the same items in the same order.
   - *remove_up_to(g : G)*—remove items in the queue until *g* is the head.

3. After we made *count* a derived query, we should have revisited earlier contracts. For example, does the contract on *remove* need changing?

4. [Harder] Develop a PRIORITY_QUEUE class. Items to be added to a priority queue need to be comparable (i.e., you can compare them using less than and greater than) so that higher priority items are retrieved from the queue first. Use the IMMUTABLE_LIST class to develop contracts for the priority queue class.

5. Rewrite the STACK class's contract using IMMUTABLE_LIST.

6. [Harder] Rewrite the QUEUE class's contract using *head : G* and *tail : QUEUE[G]*. Observe that you no longer need *items*.

Design by Contract and Inheritance

6.1 ABOUT THIS CHAPTER

This chapter explores how to write contracts in subclasses that inherit contracts from superclasses. In doing so, it

- Explains that a subclass can have a different contract from its superclass, but it must respect the superclass's contract.
- Introduces simple rules for subclassing, and then more advanced rules for reusable classes and subclassing.

6.2 SUPERCLASSES AND SUBCLASSES

When you write a subclass of an existing class, you might want to redefine some of the features of the superclass, and that might entail changing the contracts on those features.

In this chapter, we begin to explore how to write contracts when subclasses inherit from superclasses. There are two parts to the exploration. First, we look at how to inherit a contract from a superclass and safely redefine it. Then we look at how to design a superclass so that it is easier to redefine its contracts in future subclasses.

6.3 REDEFINING CONTRACTS

In this section, we start from an existing class and examine how to build a subclass that

- Inherits a contract from its superclass.
- Redefines that contract.
- Respects the inherited contract.

The example used in this section is not a software one, although it could become a software example. The example concerns a courier company that delivers packages within a city. Here is a specification of a *deliver* service, given in Eiffel. Even though we won't write an implementation in software, a specification expressed as a contract is still helpful to our discussion.

class COURIER

    feature

        deliver(p : Package, d : Destination)
            -- Deliver package to destination
          require
            -- Weight of package p does not exceed 5 kg
          ensure
            -- Package delivered within 3 working
            -- hours of when it was accepted

      ...
end

The *deliver* feature has a contract. Within that contract, the precondition places an obligation on the client of the *deliver* service not to ask for delivery of packages over 5 kg in weight. The precondition is a benefit to the supplier of the courier service, who does not have to cope with heavy packages.

The postcondition confers a benefit on the client, who can be sure that the package is delivered within 3 working hours. The postcondition places an obligation on the supplier, who must make sure that accepted packages are delivered within 3 working hours.

Table 6.1 summarizes these obligations and benefits, and shows whether they arise from the precondition or the postcondition.

What happens if the delivery service is actually provided by a different courier, a subclass of COURIER? Figure 6.1 shows the key objects and classes we need to consider.

There is a client object, *a_client*, of class CLIENT (note 1 on Figure 6.1). It makes use of a courier's *deliver* service. It thinks the *deliver* service is provided by the COURIER class (note 2). However, the courier object, *a_courier*, is not of the COURIER class. It is actually of some subclass called DIFFERENT_COURIER (note 3). So, the *deliver* service is really provided by the DIFFERENT_COURIER class. What if the precondition and the postcondition on the *deliver* service in the DIFFERENT_COURIER subclass are not exactly the same as the precondition and postcondition on the *deliver* service in the COURIER superclass? Will the client still find the *deliver* service acceptable?

We first explore what would be an acceptable precondition in the subclass and then look at the postcondition.

Table 6.1 Obligations and Benefits for Clients and Suppliers

	Client	Supplier
Obligation	Precondition Don't ask for delivery of packages over 5 kg in weight	Postcondition Deliver package within 3 working hours
Benefit	Postcondition Get package delivered within 3 working hours	Precondition Don't have to cope with packages over 5 kg in weight

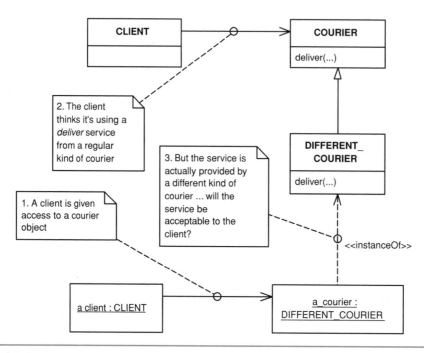

Figure 6.1 The key objects and classes involved in the delivery service

Redefining a Precondition If the *deliver* service in the DIFFERENT_COURIER subclass has the same precondition as in the superclass, then the client will be happy. In this case, if the client asks the courier to deliver a package weighing up to 5 kilograms, the courier will accept it .

Now imagine that the *deliver* service in the subclass DIFFERENT_COURIER has the following precondition (we'll discuss the Eiffel syntax in the next section):

precondition
    -- Weight of package must not exceed 8 kg

If you are the client, and you expect your courier to deliver packages up to 5 kilograms in weight, you will not mind if, unbeknown to you, the *deliver* service is subcontracted to a courier that can handle packages up to 8 kilograms in weight. All your packages, which weigh up to 5 kilograms, will be delivered.

However, now imagine that the *deliver* service in the DIFFERENT_COURIER subclass has the following precondition:

precondition
    -- Weight of package must not exceed 3 kg

If you ask the courier to deliver a package weighing 4 kilograms, you will be disappointed to find that the courier refuses to deliver it.

From this example, we can see that a subclass can have a *less* restrictive precondition than its superclass, but not a more restrictive precondition. A less restrictive precondition is often called a weaker precondition because it places a weaker constraint on the client.

A feature in a subclass can leave the precondition on an inherited feature unchanged, or it can redefine the precondition to be a weaker one.

Redefining a Postcondition   There are also three cases to consider for the postcondition on the *deliver* service in the DIFFERENT_COURIER subclass. First, if the postcondition in the subclass is exactly the same as in the COURIER superclass, the client will be satisfied.

Second, imagine that the postcondition on *deliver* in the subclass is this (again, we will give the Eiffel syntax in the next section):

postcondition
    -- Package delivered within 2 working hours

This postcondition places a stronger constraint on the supplier of the *deliver* service. A client that believes it is signing up for a delivery in no more than 3 hours will find a faster service acceptable.

For the third and final case, consider the following postcondition in the subclass:

postcondition
-- Package delivered within 5 working hours

The client will find this unacceptable. The client was expecting delivery within 3 working hours.

The examples show that a postcondition on a feature in a subclass can have the same postcondition as in the superclass, or a stronger one.

6.3.1 EIFFEL SYNTAX

As the example of the *deliver* service has shown, in order for a subclass object to fulfill the contract given in a superclass, we must redefine inherited features only in certain controlled ways.

A precondition in a subclass can be the same as, or weaker than, the inherited precondition. A postcondition in a subclass can be the same as, or stronger than, the inherited postcondition.

Eiffel directly supports these redefinition rules, and we now look at how it does so. First, a subclass that redefines an inherited feature must declare that it is going to do so. Thus, the DIFFERENT_COURIER class would begin like this:

class
DIFFERENT_COURIER
inherit
COURIER
redefine
deliver
end

feature
...

Second, the redefined contract on the *deliver* service is expressed in **require** and **ensure** clauses, but with the addition of further keywords, like this:

feature

> *deliver(p : Package, d : Destination)*
> > -- Deliver package to destination
> **require else**
> > -- Weight of package p does not exceed 8 kg
> **ensure then**
> > -- Package delivered within 2 working hours

The complete precondition on the *deliver* service in the DIFFERENT_COURIER class is this:

> *deliver(p : Package, d : Destination)*
> > -- Deliver package to destination
> **require**
> > -- Weight of package p does not exceed 5 kg
> **require else**
> > -- Weight of package p does not exceed 8 kg

The **require** is inherited from the superclass, COURIER. The **require else** part is defined locally in the DIFFERENT_COURIER subclass. The meaning of the complete precondition is as follows:

> Weight of package p does not exceed 5 kg
> **or else**
> > Weight of package p does not exceed 8 kg

Logically, this is equivalent to saying

> Weight of package p does not exceed 8 kg

Now consider what happens if we try to strengthen a precondition, for example, by restricting the weight of the package not to exceed 3 kilograms:

class DIFFERENT_COURIER

...

    deliver(p : Package, d : Destination)
             -- Deliver package to destination
        require else
             -- Weight of package p does not exceed 3 kg

The meaning of this precondition is

    Weight of package p does not exceed 5 kg
or else
    Weight of package p does not exceed 3 kg

which reduces to

    Weight of package p does not exceed 5 kg

The **require else** syntax is there to remind the reader that the redefined precondition is combined using **or else** with the inherited precondition. Because Eiffel uses **or else** to combine the original superclass precondition and the new subclass precondition, you cannot strengthen a precondition. (Stylistic note: Writing a new subclass precondition such as "-- Weight of package p does not exceed 3 kg" knowing that it will not be effective would be poor programming style.)

Now let us turn to the postcondition. The COURIER superclass defines the postcondition on the *deliver* feature to be

    ensure
             -- Package delivered within 3 working hours

In the DIFFERENT_COURIER subclass, the postcondition clause states

> *ensure then*
> -- Package delivered within 2 working hours

Taken together, they say

> *deliver(p : Package, d : Destination)*
> -- Deliver package to destination
>
> ...
> ***ensure*** *-- inherited from COURIER*
> -- Package delivered within 3 working hours
> ***ensure then***
> -- Package delivered within 2 working hours

The complete postcondition is formed using ***and then*** (an early termination version of ***and***), like this:

> -- Package delivered within 3 working hours
> ***and then***
> -- Package delivered within 2 working hours

The only way you can fulfill a promise to deliver a package within 3 hours ***and*** within 2 hours is to deliver it within 2 hours. So the postcondition is equivalent to

> -- Package delivered within 2 working hours

In other words, Eiffel's use of ***ensure then*** leads you to strengthen the postcondition.

6.3.2 SUMMARY

So far in this chapter we have seen that

- In a subclass, you can redefine a feature that is inherited from a superclass.
- As part of this redefinition, you can change the contract on the inherited feature.
- You can *weaken* the precondition.

- You can *strengthen* the postcondition.
- Eiffel uses ***require else*** and ***ensure then*** to introduce preconditions and post-conditions on redefined features, leading you to weaken preconditions and strengthen postconditions, which is what you ought to do.

6.4 INVARIANTS AND INHERITANCE

Now let us consider what it means for a subclass to respect the invariant of a superclass.

Suppose that our courier service has an insurance policy to cover claims for damage to packages in transit. The amount of this insurance is defined in an invariant on the COURIER class:

class COURIER

   ...

invariant
   insurance_cover_in_dollars >= 1000000
end

The invariant says that an object of the COURIER class has at least a million dollars' worth of insurance coverage. Informally, an invariant defines when an object is in a valid state. A courier object is in a valid state if it has at least a million dollars' worth of insurance coverage. It is in an invalid state if, for instance, it only has 100 dollars' worth of coverage. If a courier object ever got into this state, we should regard it as an invalid object and stop using it.

If an object of some subclass, such as DIFFERENT_COURIER, is to be used in place of an object of class COURIER, it must be valid in all those circumstances in which a COURIER object is valid. It might define its own invariant. But to be valid, it would need its own invariant ***and*** that of its superclass to be true. Here is an acceptable invariant in the DIFFERENT_COURIER subclass.

class *DIFFERENT_COURIER*
inherit
    COURIER

    ...

invariant
    insurance_cover_in_dollars $>=$ *2000000*
end

There is no special syntax for an invariant in a subclass. The Eiffel rules are simple. A subclass inherits its superclass's invariant, and this is **and**-ed onto any invariant clauses defined in the subclass, which is what we want.

The complete invariant in our DIFFERENT_COURIER subclass is therefore

insurance_cover_in_dollars $>=$ *1000000*
insurance_cover_in_dollars $>=$ *2000000*

and the two lines are combined by **and**, just as if they had both been written within one class.

In summary, the rule is this:

- A subclass inherits its superclass's invariant.
- It can add more clauses to the invariant, which are **and**-ed onto the inherited clauses, thus strengthening the inherited invariant.

6.5   DESIGNING SUPERCLASSES WITH GUARDED POSTCONDITIONS

So far in this chapter, we have taken the subclass's viewpoint in looking at the relationship between contracts in superclasses and contracts in their subclasses. In this section, we take the superclass's viewpoint. We explore how to write contracts in a superclass in order to make the job of redefining them in subclasses easier. Briefly, to make it easy to redefine a feature in subclasses, all postcondition clauses should be guarded by the feature's precondition.

We use a new example concerning a list of people's names. Imagine that you are designing a program that uses a list of names to decide whose turn it is to go out and buy the pizzas for lunch. Within the program, there is a NAME_LIST class. The NAME_LIST class offers a *has* feature, which returns true if a given name is already in the list. It also has a *put* feature, defined by a contract.

class NAME_LIST

    feature
        has(a_name : STRING) : BOOLEAN
            -- Is 'a_name' in list?

        put(a_name : STRING)
            -- Add 'a_name' to list
         require
            not_already_in_the_list:
                not has(a_name)
         ensure
            on_the_list:
                has(a_ name)
            number_of_names_increased:
                count = **old** count + 1

The precondition prevents a client from adding a name to the list when the name is already there. The postcondition specifies that putting a name into the list makes sure the name is there (the list *has* the given name) and increases by one the *count* of how many names are in the list.

Now imagine that you are writing a new application that needs lists of names, and that you would like to reuse class NAME_LIST. However, you want a slight variation of the *put* feature. You want to relax the precondition and allow clients to call *put* with names already in the list. When *put* is called with a name that is already in the list, it simply does nothing.

You decide to call the new class RELAXED_NAME_LIST. You define that it inherits from NAME_LIST and declare that it redefines *put*.

class
    RELAXED_NAME_LIST
inherit
    NAME_LIST
redefine
    put
end

You begin work on the *put* feature by writing its contract, which begins like this:

feature
    put(a_name : STRING)
        -- Add name to list
      require else
        already_in_the_list:
          has(a_name)

You have already inherited the precondition

        not_already_in_the_list:
          not *has(a_name)*

and, because you are allowed to weaken a precondition but not strengthen it, Eiffel does two things:

1. It combines the require clause in the superclass and the require clause in the subclass using the logical operator ***or else.***
2. It makes you use the keywords ***require else*** in the subclass as a reminder that you have inherited the superclass's require clause and you are weakening it.

The full precondition on *put* is therefore

not *has(a_name)* **or else** *has(a_name)*

which is the same as **true**. In other words, there is now no precondition on when a client can call *put*.

Here is part of what is called the *flat-short* form of your subclass (a *flat* form of a class includes the features defined locally, and those inherited from superclasses; a *short* form of a class shows you only the contracts on only the public features):

put (a_name: STRING)
      -- Add name to list
   require *-- from NAME_LIST*
      name_not_in_list:
         not *has (a_name)*
   require else
      name_in_list:
         has (a_name)

Now we turn our attention to the postcondition. Recall that, in a subclass, you are allowed to keep a postcondition the same as in the superclass or to strengthen it. Accordingly, redefined postconditions are introduced in Eiffel using **ensure then** to remind the reader that the ensure clause in a subclass is combined with that of the superclass using **and then**.

If we weaken the precondition on *put* so that it can be called with a name already in the list, we need to rethink the postcondition, which in the original NAME_LIST class was this:

ensure
   on_the_list:
      has(a_name)
   number_of_names_increased:
      *count = **old** count + 1*

It is still true that the list *has(a_name)* when called with a name already in the list. However, it is not true that the count increases. If you call *put* with a name that is already in the list, *put* simply ignores it and the *count* doesn't change. We might try to write this in the subclass's postcondition.

ensure then
    count_unchanged:
       count = **old** *count*

But this doesn't work. It gives the combined postcondition

    *(count = **old** count + 1)* **and then** *(count = **old** count)*

which is, of course, impossible to implement. You cannot make a variable increase its value *and* keep its old value.

To overcome this problem, we need to think carefully about what the original contract in the superclass really means. It means something like this:

- A client must not call the feature unless the precondition is true.
- If the client does call the feature when the precondition is true, the supplier must make sure the postcondition becomes true.

The second bullet describes the meaning of the postcondition. The meaning is conditional. The supplier is promising to make the postcondition true only if the client respects the precondition. If we express this conditional nature of the postcondition explicitly, our problem is solved.

Here is the contract on *put* in the NAME_LIST superclass, expressed conditionally.

put(a_name : STRING)
      -- Add name to list
    require
      not_already_in_the_list:
        not *has(a_name)*

> **ensure**
>   *on_the_list:*
>   (**old not** *has(a_name))* **implies** *has(a_ name)*
>   *number_of_names_increased:*
>   (**old not** *has(a_name))* **implies**
>   *count =* **old** *count + 1*

Both clauses in the original postcondition have had this added in front.

> (**old not** *has(a_name))* **implies**

As a result, each postcondition clause now has the structure

> (**old** *precondition)* **implies** *original_postcondition*

which has this meaning:

> "If the precondition was true before the feature was called then the postcondition is true when the feature has finished executing."

Returning to the name list example, here is the redefined part of the contract on the *put* feature in the RELAXED_NAME_LIST class:

put (a_name: STRING)
       -- Add name to list
    require else
       name_in_list:
          has (a_name)
    ensure then
       count_unchanged_if_name_was_already_in_list:
          (**old** *has (a_name))* **implies** *count =* **old** *count*

The precondition specifies that it is acceptable to call *put* with a name that is already in the list. The postcondition says that, when you do that, the count does not change. The postcondition is expressed in its conditional, or guarded, form.

It says that "if the name was in the list before the feature was called then the count does not change."

Now here is the complete contract on the *put* feature in the RELAXED_NAME_LIST subclass. It brings together the original contract in class NAME_LIST and the redefined part from class RELAXED_NAME_LIST.

put (a_name: STRING)
      -- Add name to list
    require *-- from NAME_LIST*
        name_not_in_list:
            not *has (a_name)*
    require else
        name_in_list:
            has (a_name)
    ensure *-- from NAME_LIST*
        count_increased:
            (old not *has (a_name))* **implies**
                        *count = **old** count + 1*
        name_in_list:
            *(**old not** has (a_name))* **implies** *has (a_name)*
    ensure then
        count_unchanged_if_name_was_already_in_list:
            *(**old** has (a_name))* **implies** *count = **old** count*

Concentrate on the two postcondition clauses that specify what the *count* is after a call to *put*. Here they are together:

      *(**old not** has (a_name))* **implies** *count = **old** count + 1*
      *(**old** has (a_name))* **implies** *count = **old** count*

Taken together they say

if
    the name was not in the list

then
    the count increases by one
else
    the count doesn't change

which is exactly what we want them to say.

The example of name lists and relaxed name lists shows that classes can be made easier to reuse if you guard each postcondition clause with the precondition. We can summarize this idea with a guideline.

> **GUIDELINE 4** To support redefinition of features, guard each postcondition clause with its corresponding precondition. This allows unforeseen redefinitions by those developing subclasses.

Of course, following this guideline entails more work. Should you always carry out that work? No, not always. When you are developing a program to a tight deadline, it does not make sense to worry much about making contracts easier to redefine in future programs. But once the program is done, and you are searching through it looking for pieces that can be put into a repository of potentially reusable classes, you will want to apply the guideline. You will sometimes also want to apply the guideline when you discover that an existing class, perhaps from another project, can be used as the superclass to a class you want to design.

6.6 TWO KINDS OF INHERITANCE

So far in this chapter, we have discussed inheritance with the assumption that objects of the subclass might be used where objects of the superclass are expected. Under this assumption, you must redefine features so that the super-class's contract is respected. In other words, you must make sure that the subclass is also a subtype. Eiffel's **require else** and **ensure then** help you achieve this goal.

There is another kind of inheritance, though. You might implement a SUB subclass by inheriting some of the features of an existing SUPER class. You might know that you will never have clients expecting the behavior defined in SUPER. Clients will only expect the behavior defined in SUB. Therefore, it does not matter whether SUB respects the contracts defined in SUPER in the ways we explained in this chapter.

Many object-oriented designers frown on using inheritance just for code reuse. However, the practice is widespread. In the bibliography, we point you to some work on using contracts to control inheritance for code reuse.

6.7 SUMMARY

If you are writing a subclass and you inherit a feature from a superclass, you can redefine its contract:

- You can weaken the precondition using ***require else.***
- You can strengthen the postcondition using ***ensure then.***
- You can strengthen the invariant simply by writing invariant clauses to be **and**-ed to those you inherited.

If you are writing a class that you expect to be used as a superclass, you can allow for a wider range of redefinitions of contracts in subclasses by guarding all postcondition clauses, so that their general form is this:

(***old*** *precondition*) ***implies*** *postcondition*

6.8 THINGS TO DO

1. Browse your Eiffel class library looking for examples of
   - Redefined preconditions
   - Redefined postconditions
   - Redefined invariants

2. Take a class from an earlier chapter (for example, the STACK class from Chapter 2) and design a subclass that redefines the contracts on some of the stack features.

3. Take a class from an earlier chapter (for example, the STACK class from Chapter 2) and rewrite its contracts using guarded postconditions.

Frame Rules

7

7.1 ABOUT THIS CHAPTER

This chapter shows how you can add frame rules to change specifications. In doing so, it

- Explains that change specifications define how commands change the values of queries and that frame rules define what does not change.
- Adds frame rules to the QUEUE class developed in Chapter 5.
- Uses the IMMUTABLE_LIST class developed in Chapter 4 to create a first version of QUEUE with frame rules.
- Uses a "forall" construct provided by a preprocessor to create a second version of QUEUE with frame rules.

7.2 CHANGE SPECIFICATIONS AND FRAME RULES

Consider this contract on the *put* routine in a SIMPLE_QUEUE class:

put(g : G)
        -- Add g to the tail of the queue

require
　　not_full:
　　　　count < capacity
ensure
　　count_increased:
　　　　*items.count = **old** items.count + 1*
　　g_at_tail:
　　　　　items.item(items.count) = g

The postcondition asserts changes to the basic queries. The first part asserts that the *count* of the number of items increases by one. The second part asserts that the item at logical position *count* in *items* is now *g*, the item being *put*.

The postcondition does not specify what does *not* change. It does not assert that putting a new item at the tail of a queue does not change the *capacity* of the queue. It does not assert that putting a new item at the tail of a queue does not change or reorder the items already on the queue.

Such assertions are important to a full understanding of the meaning of *put*. They are usually known as *frame rules*. Frame rules specify what does not change.

As a first example, we extend the postcondition of *put* to specify that the *capacity* does not change.

put(g : G)
　　　　-- Add 'g' to the queue as the oldest item
　　require
　　　　not_full:
　　　　　　count < capacity
　　ensure
　　　　count_increased:
　　　　　　*items.count = **old** items.count + 1*
　　　　g_at_tail:
　　　　　　items.item(items.count) = g
　　　　capacity_unchanged:
　　　　　　*capacity = **old** capacity*

The extra assertion checks that the implementation of *put* does not change the *capacity* of a queue.

The postcondition now contains two kinds of assertions:

1. Change specifications (the assertions tagged with *count_increased* and *g_at_tail*). These assert that certain things change.
2. Frame rules (in this case, just the assertion tagged with *capacity_unchanged*). These assert that certain things remain unchanged.

Next, we develop a more complicated frame rule to say that putting a new item onto the end of a queue does not disturb the items already there. In fact, the items already there remain the same in 3 ways:

1. The queue contains the same items as before the call to *put*.
2. These items are still in their original positions.
3. The contents of these items, which are objects, haven't changed.

We are going to explore two ways to express these frame rules:

- Using immutable lists (which were developed in Chapter 4)
- Using a purpose-built preprocessor that extends Eiffel's assertion language to allow assertions of the form "for all values of i in the range 1 to n, the following is true ... ."

7.3   FRAME RULES FOR *PUT* USING IMMUTABLE LISTS

The contract on the *put* feature in class SIMPLE_QUEUE currently looks like this:

put(g : G)
   -- Add 'g' to the queue as the oldest item
  require
   not_full:
    count < capacity

ensure

    number_of_items_increased:

        items.count = **old** *items.count + 1*

    g_at_tail:

        items.item(items.count) = g

    capacity_unchanged:

        capacity = **old** *capacity*

This contract makes use of SIMPLE_QUEUE's basic query

capacity : INTEGER

    -- Maximum number of items

the *item* and *count* properties of the basic query

items : IMMUTABLE_LIST[G] is

    -- The items in the queue, in queue order

and the derived feature

count : INTEGER

    -- The number of items in the queue

The postcondition on *put* contains one frame rule concerning *capacity*. We can add a second frame rule concerning the items in the queue by adding a fourth assertion to the postcondition on *put*. We'll present it, and then explain it.

    original_items_unchanged:

        *items.sublist(1, old items.count).is_equal(**old** items)*

To understand what the assertion says, suppose we have a queue with 10 items, and we put one more item onto the end of the queue, so that it now holds 11 items. We assert that the *sublist* containing the first 10 (i.e., **old** *items.count*) of these 11 items must equal the list containing all the items that were there before the call (i.e., **old** *items*).

The frame rule makes use of the *is_equal* query on lists. Two lists are equal if they hold the same items. This leaves open a subtle hole in the frame rule. What if two lists hold references to the same objects, but these objects are in different states? This needs some pictures to explain.

Figure 7.1 shows a list object containing three string objects. Each object has its address in memory written above it.

The same objects can be shown without explicit arrows (see Figure 7.2). It makes the picture harder to understand, but you will see that we need pictures of this kind.

Item one of the list, for example, holds the address of the first object on the right, 1001, a fact that was shown with an arrow in Figure 7.1. Using this notation, Figure 7.3 shows two lists that are equal according to the definition of the *is_equal* feature in class IMMUTABLE_LIST.

The list whose memory address is 500 is equal to the list whose memory address is 4000 because they both hold the addresses of the same objects (i.e., 1001, 2002, and 3003).

Now consider the two lists in Figures 7.4 and 7.5. They were formed at different times. Figure 7.4 shows the list whose memory address is 500 as it looked at some

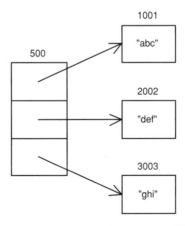

Figure 7.1 A list object containing three string objects

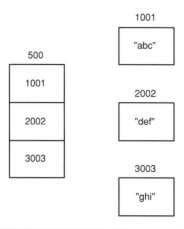

Figure 7.2 The list object shown with addresses in place of arrows

time t_1. Figure 7.5 shows the list whose memory address is 4000 as it looked at some time t_2, a little while after time t_1.

The list at 4000 holds exactly the same addresses as the list at 500, but the contents of the string object at 1001 has changed between time t_1 and time t_2. However, by the definition of *is_equal* in class IMMUTABLE_LIST, the lists at 500 and 4000 are equal. The two lists hold the same objects.

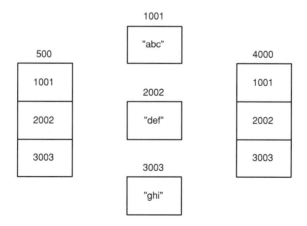

Figure 7.3 Two equal lists

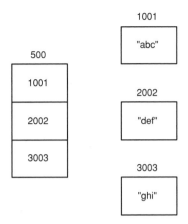

Figure 7.4 The first of two apparently unequal lists

The context for this discussion is frame rules, rules that constrain objects not to change between the time just before a call to a feature and the time just after that call. What the preceding discussion shows is that we have to be very careful about what might change. There are two properties of a list that can change quite independently: one object in the list might be replaced by another; or the contents of an object might change.

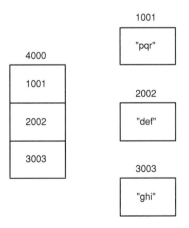

Figure 7.5 The second of two apparently unequal lists

The problem is not solved by changing the meaning of *is_equal* in class IMMUTABLE_LIST to check that the elements are equal both by "=" and by *is_equal.*

> *head = other.head*
> **and**
> > *head.is_equal(other.head)*
> **and**
> > *tail.is_equal (other.tail)*

The *items* query returns a list of addresses of the objects that are the items in the queue. If the body of *put* contains a bug and changes the contents of an item already in the queue, the list of addresses will not have changed and the test that the head of the list after the call to *put* is equal to the head before the call succeeds. At the time of the test, both *head* and *other.head* are pointing to the same object.

What we need are two separate checks:

- Does the queue after *put* contain the same objects as before *put?*
- Do these objects have the same contents as before *put?*

At present, we can only perform the first check. To be able to perform the second check, we need to keep a copy of what was in the objects in the queue before the *put,* and to compare it with what is in the objects after *put.*

We can use Eiffel's library feature *deep_clone* to help with the second check, together with *deep_equal.* Here is a postcondition on *put* that uses these two features (we'll need to make one small addition in a moment):

original_items_unchanged:
> *(deep_equal(items.sublist(1, items.count − 1),* **old** *deep_clone(items)))*

There is one last step we need to take. The check that the original items are unchanged makes sense only when there were items in the queue before the call to *put*. In fact, this applies to both frame rules: the check that the original items remain, and the check that the original items are unchanged. Both need guarding by a test for whether there were any items before the call to *put*. This guard can, for instance, test whether the size of the queue is now at least two (because, if the size of the queue is now one, it was previously empty).

Putting all the pieces together, we arrive at this contract for the *put* feature.

put(g : G) is
       -- Add g to the tail of the queue
   require
      not_full: *count < capacity*
   ensure
      number_of_items_increased:
         *items.count = **old** items.count + 1*
      g_at_tail:
         items.item(items.count) = g
      capacity_unchanged:
         *capacity = **old** capacity*
      original_items_remain:
         (items.count>=2) implies
            *(items.sublist(1, items.count − 1).is_equal(**old** items))*
      original_items_unchanged:
         items.count >= 2 implies
            (deep_equal(items.sublist(1, items.count − 1),
               ***old** deep_clone(items)))*

One of the suggestions for something to try (at the end of the chapter) is to add frame rules to the *remove* feature.

7.4 FRAME RULES FOR *PUT* USING "FORALL"

In this section, we explore two related topics:

- How a simple frame rule on the *put* feature could be expressed using the predicate logic operator "forall."
- How frame rules expressed using "forall" could be transformed into Eiffel automatically by a preprocessor.

The transformation from an assertion containing "forall" to one without "forall" is relevant in the context of other programming languages, too. For instance, the Java preprocessor we use in Chapter 11 makes the same kind of transformation.

Using "forall" in a Frame Rule We begin by formulating a simple frame rule using "forall".

In the postcondition of the *put* feature, we want to assert that the items that were in the queue are still there, and they are still in their same logical positions. Here is a first try, not yet in Eiffel-like syntax:

forall i in the range 1 to count,
    the item at position i is what was at position i before the call

We must be careful. It is actually the items indexed by values of *i* in the range 1 to the *old* value of *count* that we are interested in. Here is the assertion again, in an Eiffel-like syntax (we will cover the details of the syntax later):

original_items_unchanged:
    --// for_all i : INTEGER in 1 .. old count,
                    item(i) = old item(i)

We can read the formal assertion part as follows "for all integer values *i* in the range from 1 to the old value of count, the item at *i* equals the old item at *i*."

Automatically Transforming Assertions Containing "forall" Let's think about what would be involved in checking this assertion. We would need to store old values of *item(i)* before executing *put*, so that they could be compared with values of *item(i)* after *put* finishes executing. We know exactly which values to store away: it is those values of *item(i)* for the values of *i* in the range from 1 to the value of *count* before *put* is executed. A preprocessor could generate code to evaluate *item(i)* for the required range of values of *i* and store them in a collection object. And the preprocessor could generate code to compare values of *item(i)* after *put* has executed with these stored values. The task of making the comparison would involve a loop, in which the index variable, *i*, is incremented from 1 to the old value of *count*.

In a little more detail, the preprocessor must perform these tasks:

1. Create a collection object of the right size (which it can calculate from the start and end values of the range for *i*) and type (which it can determine from the type of *item*).
2. On entry to the *put* feature, store values of *item(i)* in this collection.
3. In the postcondition of the *put* feature, call a Boolean-valued function to compare the stored values of *item(i)* with values calculated now.

The preprocessor we used was developed for us by Chris Thomas. The preprocessor is available on the book's Web site. It has very limited capabilities; it was developed as a proof-of-concept prototype, not a working tool, and is certainly not an industrial-strength tool.

A final section of this chapter shows you in more detail what code the preprocessor generates.

Others have developed more extensive and more robust preprocessors (see the bibliography and the Web site).

7.5   KINDS OF FRAME RULES

As the UML class diagram in Figure 7.6 shows, our SIMPLE_QUEUE class has two basic queries, four derived queries, one creation command, and two other commands. Two of these nine features take a parameter.

Using SIMPLE_QUEUE as an example, we can identify several issues that frame rules could address:

- **Regular commands.** A command's job is to change the state of the receiving object, but only in certain ways. A frame rule on *put* could assert that the items already in a queue are unchanged by putting a new item at the tail.
- **Creation commands.** Before a creation command, an object is in no particular state. Thus, a creation command cannot assert that the state after the command has not changed from the state before the command (but see the parameters issue).

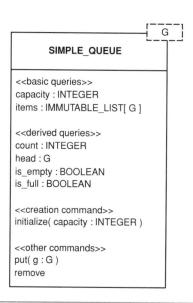

Figure 7.6 A simple queue class

- **Basic queries.** Queries are supposed to return a result but not change the state of the receiving object. For example, asking a queue for its capacity is not meant to change the capacity or change any of the items in the queue. We could add a postcondition to *capacity* to assert that calling *capacity* does not increment its value, nor change the queue's items.
- **Parameters.** Usually a routine that is passed a parameter is not meant to alter that parameter. A postcondition could be added to that effect.

Is it realistic to develop frame rules to cover all these issues? Obviously, in a throw-away prototype, the answer is no. In certain specialized situations, the answer might be yes. Imagine that you are developing a software component that will form part of the controller in every model of dishwasher your company manufactures. Fixing a bug in such a component would be horrendously expensive after large numbers of dishwashers have shipped. Catching bugs, any bugs, with extra assertions might be well worth the effort.

Between these two extremes, here is an approach suitable for many projects:

- Add frame rules occasionally, particularly where there is evidence that client programmers misunderstand what a feature does and does not do.
- Adopt a convention that all classes come with an implicit frame rule, which states that, unless a postcondition asserts that some property changes, it does not change (unexpected changes are then symptoms either of poor documentation or of bugs). The implicit frame rule can cover commands, queries, and parameters.
- In design reviews, check the code against both explicit frame rules and the implicit frame rules previously proposed.

Understanding what issues frame rules address and understanding some of the subtleties of formulating frame rules should help you check that code does not break implicit frame rules introduced by the preceding convention.

7.6 THINGS TO DO

1. Add frame rules to the contract for *remove* using both techniques: immutable lists and "forall." (Hint: You can think of removing the first element of a queue in terms of shifting all the other elements one position toward the head of the queue.)

2. Revisit the frame rule on *put* that uses "forall" and the preprocessor. Extend it to cover both "existing objects are still there, in the same positions" and "existing objects' contents don't change."

3. Add frame rules to the STACK class of Chapter 2.

7.7 APPENDIX: MORE ABOUT THE PREPROCESSOR

This section is an appendix to the chapter. It shows the gory details of the code that a preprocessor could generate to turn "forall" assertions into executable code to check the assertions. You don't have to understand the details in order to write contracts.

Here is a skeleton of the *put* feature with code that could be added by our preprocessor. Look for two methods with names beginning "*put__*".

```
put(g : G) is
        -- Add 'g' to the queue as the oldest item
    require
        not_full:
            count < capacity
    do
        put__for_all_old_1_save (g, 1 , count)
        position_of_last :=
            next_location_after(position_of_last)
        contents.put(g, position_of_last)
        count := count + 1
```

ensure
    number_of_items_increased:
        count = old count + 1
    g_is_the_youngest_item:
        item(count) = g
    original_items_unchanged:
        -- for_all i:INTEGER in 1 .. old count,
        -- item(i) = old item(i)
        put__for_all_i (g, 1 , old count)
end

The first line in the body of *put* is an automatically generated call to a procedure that stores away values of *item(i)*. The name of the procedure is generated by an algorithm that ensures uniqueness. We will examine the body of this procedure shortly.

The assertion in the postcondition containing "forall" has been turned into a comment, followed by a call to a function that returns a Boolean result (in the unprocessed version, the assertion was introduced by "--//", which acts as a signal to the preprocessor that here is a line to be processed).

The preprocessor generates the following declaration of a collection object:

put__for_all_old_1: INDEXED_COLLECTION [like item]

The type of elements in the collection is declared to be "like item", making use of Eiffel's anchored declaration facility (which allows you to declare one type to be the same as another).

The preprocessor generates the following code for the procedure that stores values in the collection:

put__for_all_old_1_save(g : G; for_all_i_from,
                for_all_i_until: INTEGER) is

```
    local
        i:INTEGER
do
    from
        i := for_all_i_from
        create put__for_all_old_1.make(for_all_i_from, for_all_i_until)
    until
        i > for_all_i_until
    loop
        put__for_all_old_1.put(item(i),i )
        i := i + 1
    end
end
```

The key line is the one that reads

put__for_all_old_1.put(item(i),i)

This stores the value of *item(i)* in position *i* of the collection.

Now here is the code generated by the preprocessor for checking values of *item(i)* in the postcondition:

```
put__for_all_i(
    g : G; for_all_i_from, for_all_i_until:INTEGER):
                                    BOOLEAN is
    local
        i:INTEGER
do
    from
        Result := true
        i := for_all_i_from
    until
        i > for_all_i_until or not Result
```

```
     loop
          Result := item(i) = put__for_all_old_1.item(i )
          i := i + 1
     end
end
```

Once again, the code is straightforward. In a loop, it compares *item(i)* now with the corresponding stored value from the collection.

Benefits of Design by Contract

8.1 ABOUT THIS CHAPTER

This chapter presents some of the benefits of using design by contract. In doing so, it

- Presents a list of benefits that was gathered by talking to people who have used contracts. We know of no industrial-scale, formal, scientific studies on the benefits.
- Compares design by contract and defensive programming.
- Presents some balancing material, looking at the costs of using design by contract.

8.2 KINDS OF BENEFITS

We have loosely categorized the benefits of using design by contract as follows:

- Achieving better designs
- Improving reliability
- Getting better documentation

- Helping debugging
- Supporting reuse

8.3 BETTER DESIGNS

The careful use of design by contract can yield designs that are better because

- The obligations of client and supplier are more clearly expressed, making designs more systematic, clearer, and simpler.
- The redefinition of features in subclasses is carefully controlled.
- Exceptions are used systematically, with a consistent meaning.

More Systematic Designs Programmers are encouraged to think about such matters as preconditions on routines because the approach makes the concept explicit.

If your programming language provides constructs for writing preconditions and then checks them at runtime, it really is easy to try using preconditions from time to time and to learn what they can do for you. You get into the habit of not leaving a class until you have checked that all the routines have their preconditions clearly expressed in *require* clauses.

Clearer Designs The obligations and benefits are shared between client and supplier and are clearly stated.

For example, in a dictionary class, can the *put(k, v)* routine deal with a key that is already in the dictionary? The designer must choose whether it is an obligation on the client not to call *put* with a key already there, or an obligation on the supplier to deal with this case, and, if so, what *put* means in this case. The contract on *put* makes the choice explicit.

Staying with the *put* routine, will *put* accept a null value? A null key? And do we know whether *value_for* might sometimes return a null value? If you are going to write code that calls features written by others, you need answers to these kinds of questions. Contracts make the answers clear.

Simpler Designs The limitations on the use of a routine are clearly expressed in its precondition, and the consequences of calling it illegally are clear, so programmers are encouraged not to build routines that are too general, but to design classes with small, single-purpose routines.

Using the dictionary example again, the *value_for(k)* routine cannot return a value for a key that is not in the dictionary, so, in principle, the client has an obligation not to call *value_for(k)* for a key not in the dictionary. This principle can be turned into practice with contracts by giving *value_for(k)* a precondition. During development, a client that calls *value_for(k)* with a key not in the dictionary receives an exception. The supplier, that is, the *value_for* routine in class DICTIONARY, is unaware of this rogue client.

Without contracts, the designer of the *value_for* routine will feel compelled to include some code in the body of the routine to defend against rogue clients. There is no longer a clean separation between pieces of program that say "here is my precondition" and pieces of code that implement the routine's functionality.

There is more on this topic in Section 8.8.

Control Over the Use of Inheritance For example, checks on contracts can ensure that, when polymorphism and dynamic binding are going to be exploited, preconditions on redefined routines are not strengthened in subclasses.

And, the close relationship between contracts and inheritance makes class designers more sensitive to the need to design classes that are open to reuse by future subclass designers.

Systematic Use of Exceptions An exception occurs when a routine is used illegally (false precondition) or when it fails to fulfill its contract (false postcondition or invariant). Exceptions thus signal faults in the code and are not an arbitrary means of transferring control used differently by different designers. This makes it easier for one person to understand another's code.

8.4 IMPROVED RELIABILITY

Contracts can improve reliability because

- The writing of contracts helps the developer understand the code better.
- Contracts help testing.

Better Understood and Hence More Reliable Code If you say the same thing twice in different ways, you will understand it better.

When you write contracts, you have to use a precondition and a postcondition to say what each routine does. And you will have to say how it does it by writing the code in its body. Having to think about the routine in two slightly different ways helps you understand more clearly what the routine does, and how. And that helps you spot faults early on.

Better Tested and Hence More Reliable Code Assertions are checked at runtime, thereby testing that routines fulfill their stated contracts.

Having contracts that can be turned on and off easily makes it easy to test and retest parts of a program. It allows you, for instance, to continue to test class A while you are working on class B, in case there are any interactions you did not foresee.

And anything that helps testing will lead to code with fewer bugs.

8.5 BETTER DOCUMENTATION

Contracts can lead to better documentation because

- Contracts are part of the public view of a class's features.
- Contracts are trustworthy documentation.
- Contracts are precise specifications that also act as test oracles.

Clearer Documentation Contracts form part of the public, or client, view of a class.

In Eiffel, for example, you write all the code in one source file. Then you use a tool to extract the client view, which contains signatures of methods and their contracts. The interface to a class is thus very clearly documented by signatures, informal comments, and supporting formal assertions.

More Reliable Documentation Assertions are checked at runtime, thereby testing that the stated contracts are consistent with what the routines actually do.

As development projects near delivery date, programmers sometimes change the code but not the documentation. When working with contracts, you can turn off assertion-checking, change the code, and leave the assertions out of date with the code. But, once you have a little time to breathe, it is an easy matter to turn assertion-checking back on and find those bits of out-of-date documentation that would otherwise be storing up trouble for later.

Explicit Test Oracle Assertions define the expected outcomes of tests and are maintained with the code.

If the postcondition on a *put* routine asserts that the *count* will increase by one, that is an expected outcome of calling *put*. And, when you run a test that includes a call to *put*, you don't have to write test code to check the outcome. If the *count* did not increase by one, there will be a postcondition failure.

Support for Precise Specifications Contracts provide a means to gain some of the benefits of precise specifications while allowing programmers to work with their familiar operational intuitions.

We need informal comments to help us build the right intuition about what the features of a class do. But then it helps to have formal documentation in a precise language to sort out the exact details of what the features do. Assertions provide just this kind of precise documentation, particularly when they are in a formal language (a programming language is, of course, formal).

8.6 EASIER DEBUGGING

Contracts can make debugging easier because they pinpoint bugs.

Support During Development Bugs that show up at runtime because an assertion evaluates to false are pinpointed with great precision.

Often, the most difficult part of debugging is locating where the fault lies. When an assertion fails, its location is precisely known.

Support During Maintenance If programs are delivered with assertion-checking switched on, customers can provide developers with more accurate information on the circumstances surrounding a failure.

This might sound an unrealistic prospect. But you can certainly give special clients prerelease versions that have lots of assertion checking still turned on. Then, when something goes wrong, they can tell you what information the runtime system supplied, and you are well on your way to finding and fixing a bug.

8.7 SUPPORT FOR REUSE

Contracts can make reuse easier by providing

- Excellent documentation
- Runtime checks that reused code is being properly used

Good Documentation for Library Users Contracts clearly explain what routines in library classes do, and what constraints there are on using them. So the power of the "not invented here" syndrome is reduced.

Help for Library Users Runtime contract-checking provides feedback to someone learning to use other people's classes.

Without contracts, if you call a library routine under the wrong circumstances, there might be no explicit feedback on what you did wrong. Well-written contracts, especially well-written preconditions, give client programmers an accurate analysis of what went wrong.

8.8   DESIGN BY CONTRACT AND DEFENSIVE PROGRAMMING

In this section, we compare design by contract and defensive programming.

We do not begin with an exhaustive study of all the different programming approaches that have been labeled as defensive. Defensive programming means different things to different people. We explore these two meanings:

- Defending a program against unwanted user input.
- Defending a routine against being called with bad arguments or when the state is inappropriate.

The second meaning, defending a routine, is explored in more detail. We discard a poor way of defending a routine. We show that better ways can be seen as implementation-level views of designs based on contracts. The mapping from designs to implementations can be used in languages that do not support design by contract, and it can be the basis of a viable approach to using contracts in concurrent and distributed programs.

8.8.1   DEFENDING A PROGRAM AGAINST UNWANTED INPUT

Checking user input is sometimes referred to as defensive programming, leading to advice like this:

> "A key defensive strategy is to check all program input. For instance, if you are asking the user to type in a date, you must check that it is a valid date."

If a program asks for a date in the form of a string, the only assumption that can be made about the input is that it is a string (assuming a strongly typed language, of course). And, if all you can assume is that the user provided a string, of course you must explore whether that string represents a date. The pieces of program that carry out this exploration might have contracts. But, if your program asks for a string, contracts cannot constrain your user only to type in strings that are valid dates.

An experienced programmer might ask for an input date by presenting a calendar from which the user can choose a date. Any rules (e.g., the date must not be in the past) can be enforced by, for example, disabling parts of the calendar. Chapter 10 shows how assertions can be used to document an informal proof that a program correctly disables screen widgets in order to enforce a rule (specifically, a precondition on a routine).

8.8.2 BULLETPROOFING A ROUTINE

In this section, we begin to explore defensive programming in the sense of protecting a routine from bad arguments. Here is an example from a card-game program. The "place card" routine places a card on a grid. The card is identified by a number, which should be in the range 1 through MAX_CARD (e.g., 52). The example is in no particular programming language.

```
placeCard(c : INTEGER, x : INTEGER, y : INTEGER) is
        -- Place card 'c' at position '(x, y)' in the grid
    do
        if (c < 1) or (c > MAXCARDS) then return -- bulletproofing
        ...
    end
```

The line with the comment "-- *bulletproofing*" does indeed defend the *placeCard* routine against a bad card number argument. The routine returns immediately if it is given a bad card number.

This kind of defensive programming is dangerous. It does defend the called routine, but it hides the possible existence of a bug in the calling code. The programmer of a calling routine that calls *placeCard* with a bad card number gets no direct feedback that anything was wrong. The problem will probably show up later in the form of evidence that does not lead directly to the source of the problem.

Whether you use design by contract or not, we recommend that you avoid writing programs in this style.

8.8.3 DEFENSIVE PROGRAMMING

As the title suggests, this section explores what we think defensive programming means. Here is the *placeCard* routine again, with one change (as before, the example is in no particular language):

```
placeCard(c : INTEGER, x : INTEGER, y : INTEGER) is
        -- Place card 'c' at position '(x, y)' in the grid
    do
        if
            (c < 1) or (c > MAXCARDS)
        then
            raise PRECONDITION_EXCEPTION(
                            "GRID:placeCard:bad card number")
        else
            ...
    end
```

This time, the *placeCard* routine raises an exception, specifically a precondition exception. The raised exception identifies the class and the routine in which the problem occurred, and the nature of the problem.

The same example written in Eiffel would look something like this:

```
placeCard(c : INTEGER, x : INTEGER, y : INTEGER) is
        -- Place card 'c' at position '(x, y)' in the grid
    require
        valid_card_number: (c >= 1) and (c <= MAXCARDS)
    do
        ...
    end
```

There is a simple, systematic mapping from the design that uses a contract to the implementation that raises an exception: each clause in the precondition becomes a statement that raises an appropriate exception if the assertion in the corresponding clause is false.

Are there any significant differences between the two versions, the one with a precondition and the one that raises an exception? Yes, there are.

First, and foremost, is the fact that the precondition is part of the documentation of the routine, whereas the statement that can raise an exception is part of the body of the routine. As a client programmer, you would have to read the implementation of the routine to discover the existence of the implemented precondition.

Of course, the routine's documentation could contain a comment to warn that there is a constraint on the card number argument. But that leads us to the second significant difference. If the constraint on the card number argument is described in a comment, there is no guarantee that the comment correctly describes the constraint (documentation is notorious for being out of date). In the version with an explicit precondition, we can trust the documentation because we are reading an assertion that is evaluated during testing. In languages without built-in support for design by contract, this advantage of checked documentation can be obtained by using a preprocessor designed to add design by contract features to the language.

We return to the theme of mapping designs based on contracts to implementations based on exceptions in Chapter 11, when we look at some examples in Java. There, in Section 11.6, we show that the mapping can be used to save expensive calls across networks.

8.9 SOME COSTS AND LIMITATIONS OF CONTRACTS

Designing programs with good contracts has associated costs: contracts take time to write, people take time to get good at writing contracts, and high quality is not always the goal. Currently, of the mainstream languages, only Eiffel supports contracts, and then only for sequential programs.

Cost of Writing Of course, it takes time to write contracts. The payback is that you save time writing test oracles, you save time writing documentation, you save time debugging, you save time when you reuse, and so on. Although most developers know that they could save time downstream by taking a bit more time on some of the upstream activities, it is still hard to resist the pressure to get on with the coding.

Takes Practice Writing good contracts is a skill. It takes time to learn to do it. If you want to make full use of contracts on your next project, you are unlikely to be given a whole team of developers who are up to speed on writing contracts, and you will have to devote project resources to training them.

Our aim in developing the set of principles and guidelines presented in this book is to reduce the time and effort others must devote to becoming good at writing contracts. And the first three chapters tell you what you need to know to begin writing very good contracts.

False Sense of Security Contracts cannot express all the desirable properties of programs. Adding contracts to programs can improve them, but it cannot make them perfect.

Quality Is Not Always the Primary Goal For some developments, the most important goal is an early release, even one with bugs. It might not help to slow down development with an activity that raises quality. (In our experience, striving for the goal of an early release of a low-quality product is usually counterproductive, but that is another story.)

Best for Sequential Programming Contracts can be used in concurrent and distributed programs. But the nature of the game changes. With design by contract, you are encouraged to design routines for clients that "look before they leap," that is, clients that make sure they fulfill the precondition before calling a routine. In a distributed system, you want routines that support "shoot first, ask questions later" clients, that is, clients who can call "try X" routines and be told after whether X was achieved. Contracts can still help in this world (see Chapter 11 for an example of transforming a design-level contract into explicit exception raising, in Java).

In addition to saving network calls, contracts warrant a second consideration in distributed systems. Some preconditions are about synchronization rather than correctness. For example, consider the precondition "buffer not empty" on a buffer's "get" routine. In a concurrent environment, whether distributed or not, the object that is getting data from a buffer might be running concurrently with an object that is putting data into the buffer. Therefore, the condition "buffer not empty" can be seen as a *wait* condition. The getting object must just wait until the putting object refills the buffer.

We know of no commercial language that supports both correctness preconditions and wait preconditions.

No Language Support If you are not working in Eiffel, you will almost certainly not have language support for contracts. There is a growing set of tools to make writing contracts easier in languages such as Java and C++. But using, for example, a preprocessor for contracts means that you are writing in one language and debugging in another, and that is always a little bit harder than working in one language.

Contracts for an Observer Framework

9

9.1 ABOUT THIS CHAPTER[1]

This chapter applies the principles and guidelines developed in earlier chapters to a small case study to explore writing contracts for a small framework derived from the observer design pattern. In doing so, it

- Shows that you can write contracts for a set of collaborating classes, as well as for individual classes such as those found in data structure libraries.

- Discusses how the contracts support extensibility (allowing subclasses to weaken preconditions without invalidating existing postconditions, and allowing subclasses to adopt different frame rules).

- Covers the privacy issues that the contracts address (ensuring that one client of a class cannot discover the identities of other clients).

- Explains that the contracts on the framework specify and check the code that is delivered with the framework. They also help to specify and check code yet to be written, that is, code that extends the framework.

---

1. The material in this chapter is based on a paper entitled "Extending a method of Devising Software Contracts" by Richard Mitchell and James McKim published in Mingins C and Meyer B (editors), *Proceedings TOOLS 32*, IEEE 1999. The material is copyright 1999 IEEE. Personal use of this material is permitted. However, permission to reprint/replenish this material for advertising or promotional purposes or for creating new collective works for resale or redistribution to servers or lists, or to reuse any copyrighted component of this work in other works must be obained from the IEEE.

9.2 THE OBSERVER FRAMEWORK

A design pattern is a design idea that has been found useful in a number of concrete designs. A framework is a design idea that has been partly implemented. To use a framework, you must understand the underlying design idea (which might be based on one or more patterns) and extend the existing implementation (for example, by writing subclasses and clients of some of the framework's classes).

The observer pattern is described in *Design Patterns* by Gamma, Helm, Johnson, and Vlissides (Addison-Wesley, 1995). It is useful when one or more objects, known as observers, need to be kept up to date with another object, known as a subject. Figure 9.1 shows the principal classes, attributes, operations, and associations in a simple version of the observer pattern.

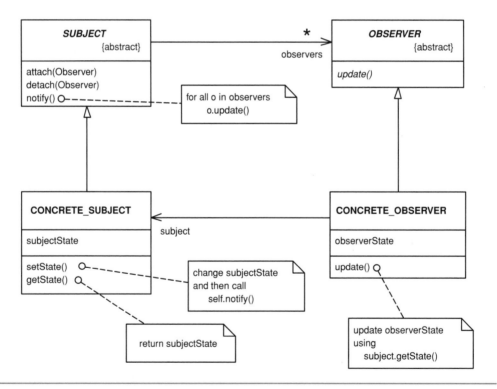

Figure 9.1 The principal elements of the Observer pattern

An observer object can *attach* itself to a subject in order to be told when to *update* itself. Each time an operation on a concrete subject changes the subject's state, it calls *notify* on itself, where *notify* is a method that the concrete subject inherits from its superclass SUBJECT. The body of *notify* calls *update* on all of the subject's currently attached observers. When an observer is told to *update* itself, it can ask for its subject's state so that it can bring its own state up to date with that of its subject.

For example, a concrete subject might be a catalog object holding a list of the items for sale in an online store. A concrete observer might manage a scrolling list in the user interface that displays the names of the items, as shown in Figure 9.2.

Almost always, we would like to avoid the catalog object's knowing how and where it is displayed. If we design the catalog to be a concrete subject, all it needs to do is to call *notify* on itself whenever its contents change. It does not know which objects get updated as a result. We then can make the scrolling list manager a concrete observer and arrange that it is attached to the catalog object. Then it will be told to *update* itself every time the catalog calls *notify* on itself.

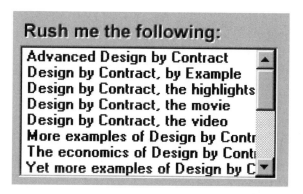

Figure 9.2 List managed by a concrete observer

Some parts of the observer pattern can be implemented without any particular application in mind, yielding an observer framework. The framework can contain

- An abstract class SUBJECT, with fully implemented features to *attach* and *detach* observers and to *notify* attached observers, but with no methods that call notify.
- An abstract class OBSERVER, with an abstract feature *update* to be effected by concrete subclasses of OBSERVER.

A designer building on this framework uses the SUBJECT and OBSERVER classes unchanged and designs application-specific subclasses to stand in the places called CONCRETE_SUBJECT and CONCRETE_OBSERVER in the pattern underlying the framework.

A framework embodies a design idea and provides some implementation. Users of a framework need to understand what the framework is providing as well as what they are expected to provide in addition. Frameworks are thus candidates for being designed, specified, and checked using the ideas of design by contract. We will develop contracts on the SUBJECT and OBSERVER classes that specify and check the implementation of the framework. Wherever possible, we write the contracts so that they also check the code that future users of the framework will develop in the subclasses.

9.3 IMMUTABLE SETS

In this chapter, we need to model the set of observers attached to a subject. We already have an IMMUTABLE_LIST class, but that is not quite what we need here. We need a set class, which provides objects that model mathematical sets. The observers attached to a subject are not going to be treated as ordered in any way. (Of course, if speed of development were critical, we could use our list class to develop version one of the observer framework and reorganize the framework later to use a set class.)

The set class we develop must provide the queries we need when writing contracts on the observer framework. This section describes a suitable set class. You might not be able to see why it is suitable until we use it to write the contracts on the observer framework in later sections. We are describing it before we need it in order to keep the description of the set class separate from discussions of how to use it in contracts on the observer framework.

Because we are going to develop a set class specifically in order to support contracts, we only need queries on set objects. We do not need any commands on set objects (other than a creation command). Therefore, we call the class IMMUTABLE_SET. Its objects cannot have their contents changed, so they are immutable.

The following fragment of Eiffel is part of the client interface to a generic class IMMUTABLE_SET. The list of features is followed by a short explanation of what they mean. Because our goal in this chapter is to write contracts on the observer framework, we do not show you the contracts for class IMMUTABLE_SET here (to find out about them, see the bibliography).

class interface IMMUTABLE_SET[G]

    count : INTEGER
        -- The number of elements in the set
    has(g : G) : BOOLEAN
        -- Is g an element of the set?
    choice : G
        -- A consistently chosen arbitrary element of the set
    clone(s: IMMUTABLE_SET [G]): IMMUTABLE_SET[G]
        -- A new set object that contains the same objects as s
    is_equal(other : IMMUTABLE_SET[G]) : BOOLEAN
        -- Does Current contain the same elements as other?
    plus(g : G): IMMUTABLE_SET [G]
        -- A new set object equal to Current with element g added
    minus(g: G): IMMUTABLE_SET[G]
        -- A new set object equal to Current with element g removed
   . . .
end -- class IMMUTABLE_SET[G]

The *count* query returns the number of elements in a set. The *has* query is the set membership test. When the expression *s.has(x)* is true, the element *x* is a member of the set *s*. The *choice* query returns an element of a set. From a client's point of view, the element is chosen arbitrarily, but consistently: a client cannot know in advance which element *choice* will return, but the choice will always be made by the same algorithm. Thus *choice* is a query, and repeated calls to *s.choice* will return the same element for as long as *s* refers to the same instance of IMMUTABLE_SET (there are no commands that can be used to change the contents of such an instance). However, the calls *s1.choice* and *s2.choice* will not necessarily return the same value when *s1* and *s2* refer to two equal, but different, immutable set objects (because the consistent algorithm will work from the set's representation, and two equal sets might not be represented identically).

The *clone(s)* query returns a new set that shares its elements with *s*. (Contrast this with a deep clone, which is a new set that contains copies of the elements of *s*, and a shallow clone, which contains a copy of whatever data structure object is used to store the elements of a set.) The *is_equal* query is the equality test corresponding to *clone*. Two sets are equal if, and only if, they contain the same elements.

The *plus* query is a functional version of the command to add an element to a set. It returns a new set containing all of the receiver's elements plus the element *g*. Similarly the *minus* query is a functional version of the command to remove an element. As we will see shortly, both *plus* and *minus* can be used in formulating frame rules, and *minus*, together with *choice*, can be used to recursively visit every element of a set.

Because every feature is a query, instances of the class are immutable. Some queries, such as *count* and *has*, return information about the current instance. Others, such as *plus* and *minus*, return new instances of IMMUTABLE_SET.

Class IMMUTABLE_SET has a creation routine, called *initialize*, which initializes a newly created set object to be empty (it ensures that *count* is zero). So, if you want to build an IMMUTABLE_SET object to represent the set {1, 2, 3}, here is how you can do it:

```
local
        s : IMMUTABLE_SET[ INTEGER]
do
    create s.initialize
    s := s.plus(1)
    s := s.plus(2)
    s := s.plus(3)
    ...
end
```

The right side of each assignment statement is an expression of the form

s.plus(i)

which creates a new set object containing all the elements of *s* and the element *i*. This newly created object is then assigned to the variable *s*, turning the previous set object attached to *s* into garbage.

9.4   ATTACHING AND DETACHING OBSERVERS

We can now begin to add contracts to the observer framework. We begin by looking at how observers are attached to subjects. (There are two complementary features, *attach* and *detach*. We will look just at *attach* because studying *detach* yields no new insights.)

When a given observer is attached to a subject, the postcondition on *attach* must assert

- That the given observer is now one of the subject's attached observers (desired change).
- That attaching this observer did not attach or detach any other observers (frame rule).

We deal first with the desired change of *attach* and then consider frame rules in Section 9.8.

To be able to formalize the assertion that *o* is an attached observer, we add a Boolean query *attached* to class SUBJECT, as follows:

attached(o : OBSERVER) : BOOLEAN
        -- Is o attached to Current?

For now, we regard *attached* as a basic query (in Section 9.7 we will make it a derived query). We can use the query in the contract on *attach* to say that attaching an observer makes it attached (postcondition), but you must not try to attach an already-attached observer (precondition). The precondition on *attach* can also address a physical constraint, in accordance with guideline G1, that the argument *o* must refer to some object.

attach(o : OBSERVER)
        -- Remember o as one of this subject's observers
    require
        exists:
            o /= Void
        not_already_attached:
            not attached(o)
    ensure
        attached:
            attached(o)

The precondition on *attach* could be removed. A discussion of whether that would improve the SUBJECT class is outside our scope, but we show how to allow for such a change in Section 9.8.

9.5 NOTIFICATION (FOR ONE OBSERVER)

When a subject changes state in a way its observers should know about, the routine that changed the state calls *notify* on itself, which will be the current concrete subject. The job of *notify* is to call *update* on each of the subject's attached observers. To simplify the presentation, we will discuss contracts for *notify* and *update* in two parts:

- Asserting that *notify* calls *update* on one of a subject's observers (this section).
- Asserting that *notify* calls *update* on all the attached observers (Section 9.6).

There is no facility in Eiffel to check that a feature has been called on some object, so there is no direct way to assert that *notify* calls *update*. However, rather than checking that *update* has been called, we can take a more problem-oriented view and check that *update* has achieved its purpose.

The point of the observer pattern is to give observers the opportunity to keep themselves up to date with their subjects in some way when their subjects change. We will work toward expressing a requirement that each observer should be up to date with its subject.

To begin with, we add a feature *up_to_date_with_subject* to class OBSERVER and use it in the postcondition of *update*, as follows:

deferred class *OBSERVER*
   . . .

   up_to_date_with_subject : BOOLEAN
       -- Is this observer up to date with its subject?

   update
       -- Bring this observer up to date with its subject
   ensure
       up_to_date_with_subject:
         up_to_date_with_subject
   . . .
end -- *class OBSERVER*

Class OBSERVER is deferred, or abstract. Each subclass of OBSERVER must provide appropriate implementations of the *up_to_date_with_subject* query and the *update* command. Providing an implementation of *update* is a normal part of using the observer framework. Providing an implementation of *up_to_date_with_subject* is an additional task, but it is a task that focuses on the reason for using the framework. (Of course, during development, you could delay implementing *up_to_date_with_subject* by providing a temporary version that returns **true** as its result.)

9.6   NOTIFICATION (FOR ALL OBSERVERS)

Now that we can check that *update* is called on one observer, we turn to the problem of checking that *update* is called on every attached observer. To perform this check, we need to be able to talk about all the attached observers. Logically, all the attached observers form a set, and we want to refer to this set within assertions. This is exactly why we introduced a class of immutable sets earlier. We can now declare the following query on class SUBJECT to allow us to talk about all the observers attached to a subject:

observers : IMMUTABLE_SET[OBSERVER]
        -- A newly created set containing the
        -- observers attached to this subject

Informally, we want a postcondition on *notify* of this form:

notify
        -- Update all attached observers
  ensure
        -- forall o in the set of observers, it holds that *o.up_to_date_with_subject*

At the time of writing, standard Eiffel does not provide a "forall" construct. So, in order to compile and test our examples, we will use an alternative approach. We will use recursion over the set of observers. An auxiliary function *all_observers_up_to_date* is introduced to handle the recursion.

all_observers_up_to_date(
    observer_set : IMMUTABLE_SET[OBSERVER]) : BOOLEAN
        -- Are all observers in *observer_set* up to date with their subjects?
    ensure
        Result =
            ((observer_set.count = 0)
            or else
                (observer_set.choice.up_to_date_with_subject)
                and
                    all_observers_up_to_date(
                        observer_set.minus(observer_set.choice))))

This function checks that all observers in a given set are up to date by checking that either

- The set is empty (the count of the number elements in the set is zero), or
- One chosen observer is up to date with its subject and, by recursion, so are all the other observers.

The consistency property of the *choice* query ensures that the element that is checked to be *up_to_date_with_subject* is the same element that is omitted by *minus* in the recursive step.

We had two reasons to make *all_observers_up_to_date* an auxiliary function with a parameter, rather than a regular query operating directly on *observers*. Doing so highlights that its role is really to provide an extension to the specification language by providing a replacement for "forall." And, at a practical level, it allows us to exploit the consistency property of *choice*.

The postcondition of notify can now use the following auxiliary function:

notify
        -- Inform all attached observers that this subject has
        -- changed by calling update on each one

ensure
>   *all_observers_up_to_date:*
>> *all_observers_up_to_date(observers)*

9.7 A PERFORMANCE ISSUE

The *observers* query is intended to support specification and checking of the observer framework. It returns an immutable set of observers as its result. An implementation of the subject side of the framework will almost certainly store its collection of attached observers in a more conventional collection class, such as an array or a linked list. The *observers* query would then be calculated from this collection, when it is needed.

The *observers* query can be used to define the *attached* query, as follows:

attached(o : ABSTRACT_OBSERVER) : BOOLEAN
>   -- Is o one of this subject's attached observers?
> *ensure*
>>   *up_to_date_with_observers:*
>>> *Result = observers.has(o)*

The *observers* query is a basic query, and *attached* is now a derived query. That means it is strictly redundant. Any use of *attached(o)* can be replaced by the expression *observers.has(o)*. However, we will retain *attached*, in line with Guideline 2 developed in Chapter 5:

> **G**UIDELINE **2** **Make sure that queries used in preconditions are cheap to calculate.** If necessary, add cheap-to-calculate derived queries whose postconditions verify them against more expensive queries.

When using Eiffel, it is common practice to develop classes with full assertion-checking turned on (to help test that the implementation is correct), but to develop clients with only precondition-checking turned on in the supplier classes (to check that the clients fulfill their side of the contract). This practice extends to the development of libraries and frameworks, such as the one under discussion.

When full assertion-checking is turned on in the observer framework, each notify cycle entails recalculating the immutable set *observers* from the underlying collection that SUBJECT uses to store its attached observers because intervening calls to *attach* and *detach* might change this collection of attached observers. In return for the benefit of extra verification, we accept the runtime penalty of using *observers* when full assertion-checking is turned on.

However, to keep the runtime penalties low when only precondition-checking is on, we allow additional, derived queries (*attached* is a good example) that are cheap to calculate. The contract for *attached* ties its result to that of the *observers* query, and this connection will thus be verified during testing, but the body of *attached* does not refer to *observers* (it calculates its result directly from the data structure SUBJECT uses to store its attached observers), and is thus cheap to execute.

There is, of course, a trade-off at work here. A user of the framework must understand each additional derived query before he or she can understand the feature it helps to specify. Adding derived queries can reduce runtime over-heads, but it can increase the intellectual load on users (although, of course, a user of the framework might find *attached(o)* easier to remember and use than *observers.has(o)*).

9.8 FRAME RULES

Frame rules are rules of the kind "and nothing else changes." Currently the postcondition on *attach(o)* asserts that observer *o* is attached. An example of a frame rule would be that attaching observer *o* does not add any other observers to the set of observers, nor remove any existing observers from it.

To capture such a frame rule, we can add an assertion to the postcondition of *attach*, such as this one, which asserts that, after *o* has been attached, the set of observers minus this newly attached observer is the same as the set of observers before the *attach*.

*observers.minus(o).is_equal(**old** (observers))*

In other words, after attaching a new observer, removing it again takes you back to exactly the set of observers you had before.

Frame rules can overconstrain developers of subclasses. For example, suppose that a subclass designer wants to extend *attach* so that, when some limit on the number of observers is reached, the oldest observer is detached to make room for the new observer. The preceding frame rule that attaching observer *o* does not add or remove any other observers would preclude the subclass designer from extending our version of *attach*.

However, if we can keep frame rules separate from change specifications, we allow a future subclass designer to abandon our frame rules but keep our change specifications (or vice versa).

Taking the subject side of the observer pattern as an example, we write non-frame contracts in one class, which contains no implementation code. We call this class SUBJECT_TYPE (see Figure 9.3). We next write the frame rules in a subclass, still with no implementation. This subclass further constrains the contracts it inherits from its superclass. We call this class SUBJECT_TYPE_WITH_FRAMING. Finally we write the implementation code in class ABSTRACT_SUBJECT, which implements the contracts it inherits. Regular users of the framework write their class in place of what we are calling CONCRETE_SUBJECT (they extend the implementation provided in ABSTRACT_SUBJECT).

A developer who wants to step outside the constraints imposed by the frame rules can replace SUBJECT_TYPE_WITH_FRAMING and make appropriate changes to the code in ABSTRACT_SUBJECT.

The approach is summarized in this guideline:

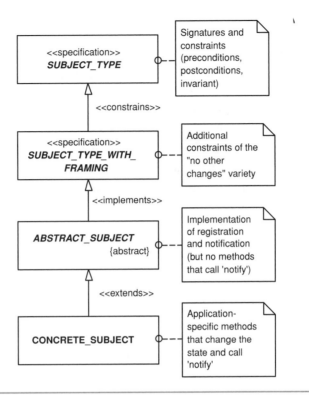

Figure 9.3 Adding frame rules to the subject type

> **GUIDELINE 5   Place constraints on desired changes and frame rules in separate classes.** This allows developers more freedom to extend your classes.

You might be thinking that adding frame rules goes beyond what is reasonable, even without the additional overhead of putting them in a separate class. For many programs, we would agree. Here, though, we are discussing a framework to be used many times in many places. In this case, the cost of providing high-quality contracts will be spread over the many beneficiaries of this extra care—all the programmers who build programs using the framework.

9.9 PRIVACY

The *observers* query was introduced to support contracts, and it is used in several assertions. The query responds with a set of all the currently attached observers.

There can be applications of the observer framework in which one observer of a subject should not be allowed to learn the identities of other observers, yet the *observers* query lets any client of a subject do just that. If privacy is needed, that is, if one observer must not be able to learn the identities of other observers, there is a straightforward solution: provide deferred classes in which *observers* is visible, and available at runtime to support checking, but hide the query before reaching the level of concrete classes.

To achieve this, the set of layers needed on the subject side of the framework is extended by one, as shown in Figure 9.4. We add the middle layer, called SUBJECT_TYPE_WITH_FRAMING_AND_VISIBILITY_CONTROL, in Figure 9.4. Once again, you might look at the figure and decide that such complications are never going to be practicable. And again, for most software, we would agree. What we are showing you is just how meticulous you can be. There are some kinds of software for which this level of care is appropriate. Examples include software that can affect lives, where the consequence of failure is potentially fatal, and software to be embedded in consumer products, where the cost of recall is prohibitively high.

In Eiffel, the relevant class looks like this:

deferred class
    SUBJECT_TYPE_WITH_FRAMING_AND_VISIBILITY_CONTROL

inherit
    SUBJECT_TYPE_WITH_FRAMING
        export *{NONE} observers* **end**

end *-- class SUBJECT_TYPE_WITH_FRAMING_AND_VISIBILITY_CONTROL*

The class inherits from SUBJECT_TYPE_WITH_FRAMING and makes the *observers* query visible to none of the possible client classes.

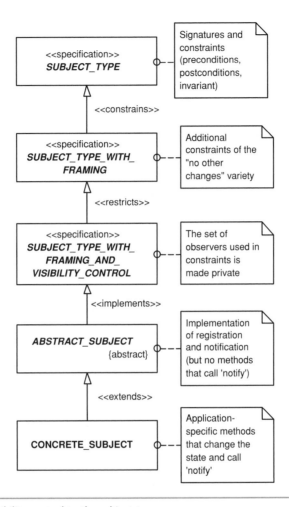

Figure 9.4 Adding visibility control to the subject type

Generalizing, we get

GUIDELINE 6   If there are privacy requirements, queries that compromise privacy can be used in contracts, and then made private. The phrase "then made private" means they are made private in layers below the one in which they are used in contracts, but above the layers to which clients have full access.

Privacy control of this kind is not without a price. The SUBJECT_TYPE_WITH_FRAMING_AND_VISIBILITY_CONTROL class is a subclass of SUBJECT_TYPE_WITH_FRAMING, but it is not a subtype because it cancels the *observers* query. A subclass that is not also a subtype needs introducing and using with care. (Indeed, many object-oriented languages will not allow you to "cancel" an inherited feature.) However, we are going to be careful, by making it clear who should be permitted to do what.

There are meant to be two kinds of users of the observer framework, whom we call regular users and reusers. Regular users import into their projects all the classes in the layers shown in Figure 9.4 except the CONCRETE_SUBJECT class, which is where they place the class that is to be a subject in their application. The imported framework code declares variables of class ABSTRACT_SUBJECT, and regular users declare variables of their own concrete subject and observer classes. There is no need to declare variables of, for instance, SUBJECT_TYPE, so there is no source of problems arising from the use of dynamic binding in the presence of canceling.

Some users will do more than use the framework. They will take it apart and reuse some of the parts. They might, for example, change some of the frame rules and adapt the implementation code accordingly to offer different functionality to regular users. Reusers who adapt the framework must understand where and why the framework has nonsubtype inheritance relationships if they are to reuse parts of the framework safely.

9.10 THINGS TO DO

1. Explore the contracts on class IMMUTABLE_SET (available from the book's Web site).

2. This chapter has presented fragments of the contracts needed on the observer framework. Complete the contracts.

3. If you haven't already done so, extend the contracts on the framework to allow for redefinitions in subclasses (as described in Chapter 6).

4. [Harder]. We have not discussed whether reentrant calls to *attach* and *detach* are allowed. An example of a reentrant call would be a call to *detach* occurring

during the life of an execution of *notify*. Such a call could detach an existing observer just before a subject calls *update* on that observer. Add the necessary features and contracts to allow someone who reads your version of SUBJECT to be sure that reentrant calls are allowed, and modify the program accordingly. The body of *notify* could begin by making a clone of the set of observers. Calls to *detach* won't disturb the clone. But how does the contract on *detach* show that an observer can still be called after being detached?

Fulfilling a Precondition

10.1 About This Chapter

This chapter distinguishes among fulfilling a precondition, testing a precondition, and checking a precondition. In doing so, it

- Defines the three terms as follows:
    - If a client calls a feature in a supplier when the feature's precondition is true, the client has *fulfilled* the precondition.
    - If code in the client evaluates the precondition prior to calling the feature, in order to be sure the precondition will be fulfilled, the client has *tested* the precondition.
    - If precondition-checking is turned on in the supplier, so that code in the supplier evaluates the precondition, the supplier has *checked* the precondition.
- Uses short examples to explain the differences among fulfilling, testing, and checking a precondition.
- Uses a larger example to show that contracts can capture the argument that a client correctly fulfills a precondition and has no need to explicitly test it.

10.2   THE EXAMPLES

Whenever a client object calls a feature on a supplier object, the client must *fulfill* any obligations placed on it by the precondition for that feature. Crucially, the client is not obliged to explicitly *test* the precondition before using the service.

The main example presented in this chapter concerns a tiny application that provides the user with a counter that has buttons with which to increment and decrement. The example illustrates the difference between fulfilling a precondition and explicitly testing a precondition. The design of a client of a feature is accompanied by an argument that the client always fulfills the precondition on the feature, so no explicit test is needed.

The argument that a client fulfills a supplier's precondition can be presented just as informal documentation. This chapter shows that we can do better than that. The argument can be expressed using contracts, so that it is more formally presented and so that it is checked during development.

Before exploring the main example, we use simpler examples, based on stacks and queues, to explore the ideas of fulfilling, testing, and checking preconditions.

10.3   FULFILLING AND TESTING A PRECONDITION

Imagine that we are working on a program that includes a queue of characters. Three key features of the QUEUE class are a feature to *put* an item into a queue object, a feature to inspect the *item* at the head of a queue, and a feature to *remove* the item at the head of the queue.

Some part of the program has filled the queue with characters. We have the task of emptying the queue onto an output stream called *out*. The following loop is the basis of our design:

from
> ...
until
> q.is_empty

loop
    out.put_char(q.item)
    q.remove
end

In class QUEUE, the *item* feature and the *remove* feature both have this precondition:

require
    not_empty: **not** *is_empty*

Any client of the QUEUE class must take care to *fulfill* this precondition when calling *item* or *remove*. Our code is a well-behaved client from this point of view. Each time around the loop, it *tests is_empty* and only proceeds into the body of the loop if *is_empty* is false. When, in the body of the loop, the client calls *item* and *remove*, we can be sure that their preconditions are being fulfilled. The client will never call *item* or *remove* when *is_empty* is true.

In this example, a client made sure it fulfilled a supplier's precondition by explicitly testing the precondition. In other examples, this explicit test might not be necessary.

As a second example, imagine we are working on a program that handles coded messages in which all characters occur in five-letter blocks. One step in the encryption process involves reversing the characters in a block. Here is how we do it in our first, prototype version of the program (in this code fragment, *s* is a stack object and *b* is a five-letter block):

```
-- Put the block's 5 characters on the stack
s.put(b.item(1))
s.put(b.item(2))
s.put(b.item(3))
s.put(b.item(4))
s.put(b.item(5))

-- Unstack them again into the block
b.put(s.top, 1)
```

s.remove

b.put(s.top, 2)

s.remove

b.put(s.top, 3)

s.remove

b.put(s.top, 4)

s.remove

b.put(s.top, 5)

s.remove

Let's concentrate on the second part of the algorithm. In this part, we repeatedly inspect the *item* on the top of the stack and put it into the i-th location in the block, and then *remove* it from the stack. There is no explicit *test* that the stack is not empty when we call *item* and *remove*. Nevertheless, the algorithm always *fulfills* the precondition on *item* and *remove*, that *is_empty* is false, because we know that the stack contains five items—the first five lines of code put them there.

What these two examples have shown is that, when a client *fulfills* the precondition on a supplier's feature, it might or might not need to explicitly *test* the precondition.

10.4 TESTING VERSUS CHECKING

In the previous section, we looked at two examples in which a client fulfilled a precondition on a supplier. In the first example, the client explicitly tested the precondition. In the second example, the client did not need to test the precondition.

Quite separately from whether a client does or does not *test* a precondition, a feature in a supplier might *check* that its clients are well behaved by checking its precondition each time it is called. In Eiffel, this checking can be turned on and off by means of a compile-time or runtime switch.

There are thus two occasions on which a precondition might be evaluated. It might be evaluated because a client *tests* the precondition as part of a correctly working algorithm. And it might be evaluated because precondition-*checking* is turned on in the supplier. (Of course, programmers only write the code for one of these evaluations, the client-side *test*. The compiler writes the code for the supplier-side *check* based on a precondition we wrote.)

We now have three separate concepts: fulfilling, testing, and checking.

- A client ought to *fulfill* a precondition.
- A client might or might not *test* a precondition in order to be sure it is fulfilling the precondition.
- A supplier might or might not *check* a precondition in order to be sure that the client did fulfill the precondition.

We are now ready to look at a more complicated example in which a client *fulfills* a precondition without needing to test it. (Whether the supplier checks it just depends on whether precondition-checking is turned on or not).

The example points out that the designer of the application can construct an argument that the client fulfills the precondition and thus does not need to test it, and that this argument is itself captured in assertions.

10.5 A SIMPLE COUNTER CLASS

Figure 10.1 is an outline design for a very simple class COUNTER, which is at the heart of the example.

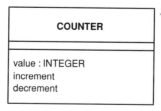

Figure 10.1 A simple counter class

You can *increment* and *decrement* an object of class COUNTER and ask it for its *value*. Here is the contract for the *decrement* routine:

decrement
      -- Decrement the value of the counter
   require
      value_is_positive:
         value >= 1
   ensure
      value_decremented:
         *value = **old** value – 1*

The routine has a precondition. A counter can be decremented only if its value is strictly greater than or equal to 1.

The class has an invariant: that the *value* of a counter is never negative. The precondition on *decrement* helps make sure that the invariant is preserved.

The precondition imposes an obligation on clients not to call *decrement* when the value of the counter is already 0. To see how a client might fulfill this obligation, we need to extend the example to include a client. We will build a small, but complete, program that includes a counter. The example program is a toy one. However, it does show how assertions can help to document an argument that one part of a program is a valid client of another part.

The next section shows the user's view of the example program. That is followed by an outline of the program's internal structure and workings. Then we are ready to develop and document the argument that the precondition on *decrement* is respected by the part of the program that uses it.

10.6 THE USER'S VIEW OF THE PROGRAM

The example program displays a window containing buttons to increment and decrement a counter and a text field to display the current value of the counter (see Figure 10.2).

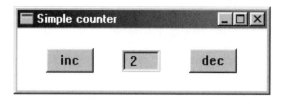

Figure 10.2 The user's view of a counter with value 2

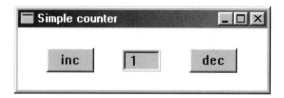

Figure 10.3 The counter after one click on the decrement button

If the user were to press the decrement button now, the counter's value would go down to 1, and the window would look like Figure 10.3. Another press on the decrement button would leave the window looking like Figure 10.4.

Notice particularly that the decrement button is grayed out when the counter's value is 0. You will have guessed, of course, that this is how the program makes sure it fulfills the precondition on the counter's *decrement* routine. It prevents the user from asking to decrement a counter that is already on 0.

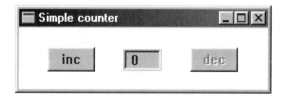

Figure 10.4 The counter on zero, with a grayed-out decrement button

There is still work to do. We need to construct an argument that the program always disables the "dec" button whenever the counter is 0. To develop this argument, we need to explore the program's internal structure and workings.

10.7 THE INTERNAL STRUCTURE OF THE PROGRAM

Figure 10.5 shows the key classes in the source code of the program. The core of the program is an object of class COUNTER, which provides routines for clients to *increment* and *decrement* the counter and to inspect its *value.*

Class COUNTER has three clients, INCREMENT_BUTTON, DECREMENT_BUTTON, and VIEW_OF_COUNTER classes.

Class COUNTER is a subclass of SUBJECT in the sense of the Observer pattern originally described by Gamma, Helm, Johnson, and Vlissides in their book *Design Patterns* (Addison-Wesley, 1995).

The associated class OBSERVER has two subclasses: VIEW_OF_COUNTER and DECREMENT_BUTTON. The text view of the counter that appears between the two buttons is an object of class VIEW_OF_COUNTER. Its contents are updated via the notify mechanism of the Observer pattern whenever the value of the counter changes.

The decrement button is also an observer of the counter. It disables itself, and hence appears grayed out, whenever the counter reaches 0, and enables itself again whenever the counter moves off 0. Like the text view, the decrement button is notified that the counter has changed its value via the notify mechanism of the Observer pattern. (The routine *on_subject_changed* is called "update" in the original description of the Observer pattern.)

The class diagram in Figure 10.5 also shows that the two button classes inherit from WEL_PUSH_BUTTON. (The abbreviation WEL stands for Windows Eiffel Library.)

Further details of the classes are discussed in the context of the program's behavior, in the next section.

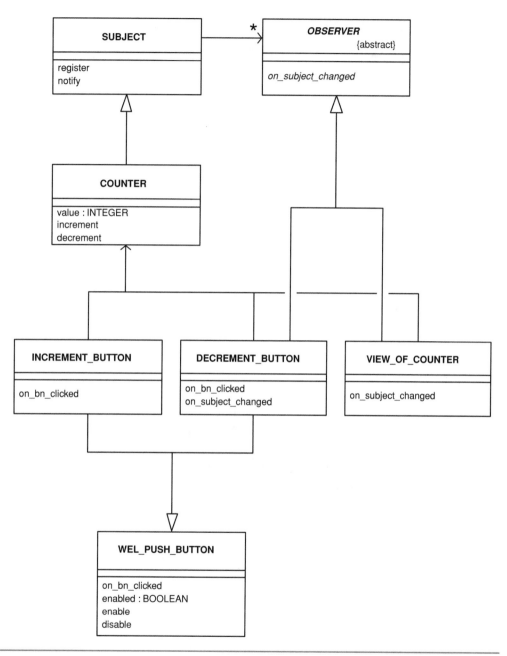

Figure 10.5 The key classes in the counter program

10.8 THE PROGRAM'S BEHAVIOR

The class COUNTER provides routines for clients to *increment* and *decrement* the *value* of the counter. We are interested in the *decrement* routine, which is listed here, with its contract and its body:

decrement
        -- Decrement the value of the counter
   require
      value_is_positive:
         value >= 1
  do
      value := value - 1
      notify
  ensure
      value_decremented:
         *value = **old** value - 1*
  end

The body decrements the value of the counter and calls *notify*. The *notify* routine is inherited from class SUBJECT because the program's counter is a subject in the sense of the Observer pattern. It is a responsibility of routines in subclasses of SUBJECT to call *notify* when they change the state of the object. The body of *notify* calls *on_subject_changed* on all registered observers of the subject (in this case, the text view of the counter and the decrement button).

The Windows Eiffel Library class WEL_PUSH_BUTTON provides the means to *enable* and *disable* (or gray out) a button and to test whether a button is currently *enabled*. Its *on_bn_clicked* routine has an empty body. Subclasses of WEL_PUSH_BUTTON that want a button to have a particular behavior must provide an implementation of the *on_bn_clicked* routine, which is called by the WEL event loop whenever the user clicks the button on the screen.

The two buttons that actually appear on the screen are objects of classes INCREMENT_BUTTON and DECREMENT_BUTTON, respectively. We will concentrate on the decrement button. It has two key routines: it implements *on_bn_clicked* because it is a subclass of WEL_PUSH_BUTTON and it implements *on_subject_changed* because it is a subclass of OBSERVER.

The implementation of *on_subject_changed* in class DECREMENT_BUTTON is as follows:

on_subject_changed is
        -- (Called by this observer's subject
        -- whenever the subject, a counter, changes.)

        -- If the associated counter is zero, disable myself.
        -- If the associated counter is nonzero, enable myself.
    do
        if
            counter.value = 0
        then
            disable
        else
            enable
        end
    ensure
        enabled_status_is_consistent_with_counter_value:
            enabled = (counter.value > 0)
    end

This routine has no precondition; it can always be called. Its postcondition asserts that the button is enabled if the counter is positive, but disabled (or grayed out) if the counter is 0. When the decrement button is disabled, the user can click the mouse over it but the GUI's event loop will ignore such clicks. In particular, the event loop will not generate a call to the button's *on_bn_clicked* routine.

The creation routine *initialize* in class DECREMENT_BUTTON also has the same assertion in its postcondition:

ensure
>enabled_status_is_consistent_with_counter_value:
>>*enabled = (counter.value > 0)*

No other routines in class DECREMENT_BUTTON change the *enabled* state of the button. Therefore, whenever the button is enabled, the counter's *value* must be greater than 0.

The code for *on_bn_clicked* in class DECREMENT_BUTTON is as follows:

on_bn_clicked is
>-- (Called by the GUI event loop.)

>-- Decrement the counter.

require
>enabled:
>>*enabled*

do
>**check** *enabled = counter.value > 0* **end**
>>-- Whenever a DECREMENT_BUTTON is
>>-- enabled, the associated counter must be
>>-- positive - see postconditions
>>-- on 'initialize' and 'on_subject_changed'.
>*counter.decrement*

ensure
>value_of_associated_counter_decremented:
>>*counter.value = **old** counter.value − 1*

end

(This version of *on_bn_clicked* is slightly simplified from the actual implementation. The differences do not affect the discussion. They are explained in Section 10.9.)

The body of the *on_bn_clicked* routine is a single statement that calls *decrement* on the counter object. The routine has a precondition that the button is *enabled*. We have just been through an argument that, when this precondition is satisfied, the counter's *value* must be positive. Therefore, every call from *on_bn_clicked* to *decrement* is valid.

The body contains a check instruction (this is the first time we have met a check instruction). The check instruction is placed before the call to *decrement*. It documents the relationship between *enabled* and the counter's *value* and provides a runtime check on the relationship. Taken together with the precondition that the button is *enabled*, it establishes that the counter's *value* is positive, so the call to *decrement* the counter respects the precondition on *decrement*.

To illustrate the interaction between the various objects, Figure 10.6 shows a sequence diagram for an important scenario in which the decrement button changes from being enabled to being disabled. This happens if a user clicks the decrement button when the counter's *value* is 1. (The sequence diagram does not include updating the text field that shows the user the *value* of the counter because that does not affect the argument.)

In detail, Figure 10.6 shows this scenario:

Initial situation   The counter's *value* is 1, and the button labeled "dec" is enabled.

Step 1   The fun begins when the user clicks the "dec" button.

Step 2   When the user clicks the "dec" button, the GUI event loop calls *on_bn_clicked* on the decrement button object.

Step 3   The decrement button's *on_bn_clicked* routine calls the counter's *decrement* routine.

Step 4   Because the counter is a subject, it calls *notify* on itself.

Step 5   The counter's *notify* routine calls *on_subject_changed* on the counter's observers, which include the decrement button.

Step 6   The decrement button checks the counter's *value*.

Step 7   Because the counter's *value* is now 0, the button disables itself.

Final situation   The counter's *value* is 0, and the decrement button is disabled.

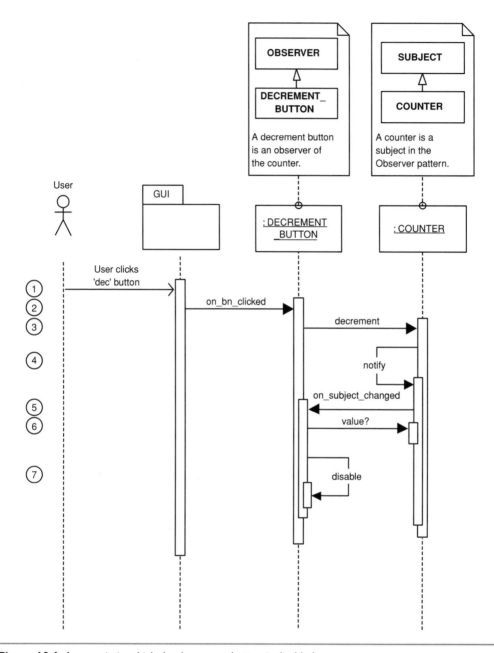

Figure 10.6 A scenario in which the decrement button is disabled

Here is a summary of the part of the contract between DECREMENT_BUTTON and COUNTER that we have been exploring:

- COUNTER exports a routine *decrement,* which must not be called when the counter is 0.
- DECREMENT_BUTTON is a client of COUNTER. It calls *decrement* from within its *on_bn_clicked* routine.
- The *initialize* and *on_subject_changed* routines in class DECREMENT_ BUTTON both have postconditions that ensure that a decrement button is *enabled* only when its associated counter's *value* is positive, and is disabled when the counter is 0.
- The *on_bn_clicked* routine has a precondition *enabled* to capture the fact that it is not called when the button is disabled (grayed out).
- The check instruction in *on_bn_clicked* brings together the two previous points in this list. Together, they tell us that when the precondition on *on_bn_clicked* is true, the counter's *value* must be positive. Therefore, the call to *decrement* from within *on_bn_clicked* is valid.

And here is the most important point of all:

The key facts in the argument are captured in assertions.

Specifically, the key facts are captured in

- The precondition on *decrement* in class COUNTER
- The postconditions on *initialize* and *on_subject_changed* in class DECREMENT_BUTTON
- The precondition on *on_bn_clicked* in class DECREMENT_BUTTON
- The check instruction in the body of *on_bn_clicked* in class DECREMENT_BUTTON

Because the key facts in the argument are captured in assertions, they can be checked at runtime as the application is developed. This cross-checking of code increases our confidence that

- The code does what the documentation says.
- The documentation is up to date, and correctly describes the code.

10.9 A MINOR DETAIL

The Windows Eiffel Library used in the example program work defines *on_bn_clicked* in deferred class WEL_BUTTON with a precondition and an empty body.

```
on_bn_clicked is
        -- Called when the button is clicked
    require
        exists: exists
    do
    end
```

The routine is designed to be redefined in subclasses. The Eiffel rules for redefinition permit a precondition to be weakened (using the ***require else*** construct), but not strengthened.

The contract for *on_bn_clicked* is not fully stated. There is an additional, implicit precondition, "button is enabled," that is respected by the client of *on_bn_clicked* (the client is the runtime system's event loop). To support our argument that the decrement button is a valid client of the counter object, we want the full precondition made explicit. To make it explicit, we need to finish writing the precondition on *on_bn_clicked*. (We are not changing the precondition—in particular, we are not strengthening it. We are just finishing the work of the library designers by writing down more of the precondition that clients are already respecting.)

We can make the full precondition explicit by forwarding calls received by *on_bn_clicked* to a locally defined routine with the full precondition, as follows:

on_bn_clicked **is**
        -- (Called by the WEL event loop, provided the
        -- button is enabled.)

        -- Forward the call to 'protected_on_bn_clicked'.
    do
        protected_on_bn_clicked
    end

protected_on_bn_clicked **is**
        -- Decrement the associated counter.
    require
        enabled:
            enabled
        associated_counter_is_positive:
            counter.value >= 1
    do
        -- My precondition implies the
        -- precondition on 'decrement'
        counter.decrement
    ensure
        value_of_associated_counter_decreased:
            *counter.value = **old** counter.value – 1*
    end

We have broken the rules for redefining preconditions because we now have a
stronger precondition on *protected_on_bn_clicked* than the precondition we
inherited on *on_bn_clicked*. However, if we concentrate on the *total* precondition, not just the stated precondition, we have made no change at all. In the
superclass, WEL_BUTTON, there was an implicit, unstated precondition on its
on_bn_clicked routine that the button is enabled. In our subclass, DECREMENT_
BUTTON, we have used the simple technique of forwarding a call to allow us to
make the precondition explicit. Then we have added a second clause, that the
associated counter's value is positive, which is just a logical consequence of the
first. So, at a logical level, we have not changed the precondition.

If you choose to develop very carefully written contracts in programs that use library classes with implicit contracts, you will find yourself using techniques like the one shown here.

10.10 SUMMARY

At this point, you could be forgiven for asking whether it could ever be worth all the effort it takes to develop the contracts described in the preceding sections.

First, the effort is not as great as it might seem. It takes a lot more time and space to explain how assertions support checking that a call is valid than it does to use it in practice. The whole argument about the correctness of the decrement button is captured in just a handful of assertions. Writing a handful of assertions is no more time consuming than writing a handful of lines of imperative code. And you do get better at devising and writing contracts with practice.

Second, the assertions and associated comments capture an argument that must be constructed by the program's designer, and must be understood by anyone reviewing the program or modifying it later. What we have shown in this chapter is that design by contract can be used to help record and check the argument.

The story does not end here. Closer inspection of the argument that DECREMENT_BUTTON is a correct client of class COUNTER's *decrement* routine shows that it relies on facts that have not been covered here. It relies on the GUI library behaving properly and not generating calls to *on_bn_clicked* for grayed-out buttons, and it relies on the proper working of the Observer pattern. The contracts we have discussed would help detect faults in this infrastructure (although none showed up during the development of the example program). And, of course, contracts in the GUI and Observer pattern classes themselves provide further checking (contracts on the Observer pattern were explored in Chapter 9).

10.11   THINGS TO DO

1. To keep the explanation simple, we didn't talk about contracts on the Observer pattern in this chapter. Download the source code for the counter application, and add contracts for the Observer pattern, using the ideas of Chapter 9.

2. [Harder] Again, to keep things simple, we focused on the contracts that show that the decrement button is a well-behaved client of the COUNTER class. We did not look at the classes independently and make sure we had applied the six principles. Apply the six principles to the counter, increment button, and decrement button classes.

11

Java Examples

11.1 ABOUT THIS CHAPTER

This chapter reworks two Eiffel examples in Java, the class QUEUE from Chapter 5 and the class DICTIONARY from Chapter 3. In doing so, it

- Uses a preprocessor called iContract to provide design by contract facilities in Java.

- Introduces the iContract syntax for assertions in the QUEUE example.

- iContract provides the universal quantifier, *forall*. The QUEUE example uses this operator and therefore does not need the IMMUTABLE_LIST class developed in Chapter 4.

- Shows how to use Java interfaces to capture contracts in the DICTIONARY example.

- Discusses how to proceed if you want at least precondition-checking in Java without a preprocessor.

- Uses the idea that a design based on contracts can be mapped to an implementation that raises exceptions. This idea was introduced in Chapter 8, on the benefits of contracts.

- Continues the distinction among fulfilling a precondition, testing a precondition, and checking a precondition that was introduced in Chapter 10 in an example in which a client fulfilled a supplier's precondition.

11.2 WHY JAVA?

Most of the examples in this book are presented in Eiffel because Eiffel was designed with facilities to support design by contract. A number of people have built tools to add design by contract facilities to other object-oriented programming languages such as C++ and Java. We want to show you examples of using one such tool, and we choose to do so using Java because

- Java is a popular language and is easy to read.
- Java has a widely accepted convention for adding documentation to source code, and contracts can be seen as extensions of conventional documentation.
- Java has interfaces, a construct not explicitly provided in earlier object-oriented programming languages such as Eiffel, Smalltalk, and C++. One of our examples shows how to present contracts without revealing which class(es) implement them.
- Java has an exception mechanism, which allows us to show you how you might incorporate a limited form of design by contract into a language that does not support it.

If you work with a language other than Eiffel or Java, we hope you will be able to carry the lessons over.

11.3 QUEUES

Figure 11.1 shows the final design from Chapter 5 for a QUEUE class to be implemented in Eiffel. Here are the changes we will make to this design in moving from Eiffel to Java:

- We will call the class *Queue* (just to have a slightly different name).
- Because this our first Java example, we will simplify the design by omitting the *capacity* and *is_full* features.
- Instead of Eiffel's *initialize* command, we will have a *Queue* constructor function.
- We will change some names to be nearer to Java naming conventions. For instance, we will have a *size* query in place of the *count* query.

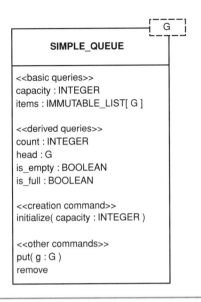

Figure 11.1 The simple queue class from Chapter 5

- We will adopt Java's convention of *namesWithCapitals*, rather than Eiffel's convention of *underscores_in_names*.

- It is not good practice to make variables visible in Java. In addition, Java functions need brackets even when they take no arguments. Therefore, we will refer to, for instance, *size()* rather than to *size*.

- We will use iContract's universal quantifier, so we will not need the immutable list *items*. Instead, we will work with a *get(int i)* query, which returns the item at position i in the queue. By quantifying over i, we will be able to assert properties of many items.

- In removing *items* as a basic query, we will need to make *size()* a basic query in order to know the range of values that *get(i)* is defined for.

- Java does not have generic classes. Java collection classes are often defined to accept objects of class *Object*, which is at the top of the class hierarchy. We will follow this convention.

- To specify the *remove()* command, we will refer to a copy of the queue, specifically a shallow copy. So we will introduce a *shallowCopy()* query (a shallow copy of a collection shares its elements with the original collection).

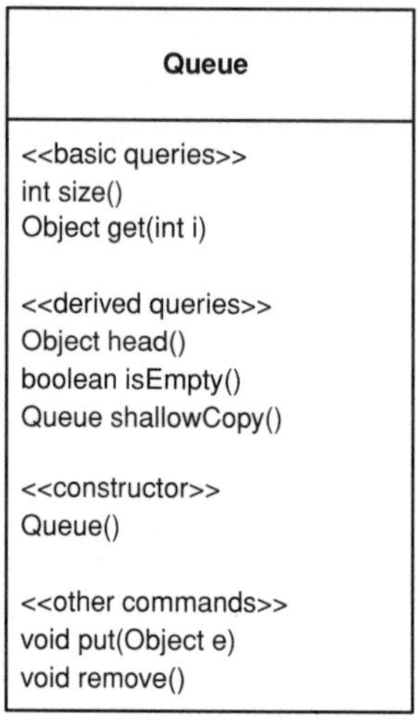

```
                    ┌─────────────────────────────┐
                    │            Queue            │
                    ├─────────────────────────────┤
                    │  <<basic queries>>          │
                    │  int size()                 │
                    │  Object get(int i)          │
                    │                             │
                    │  <<derived queries>>        │
                    │  Object head()              │
                    │  boolean isEmpty()          │
                    │  Queue shallowCopy()        │
                    │                             │
                    │  <<constructor>>            │
                    │  Queue()                    │
                    │                             │
                    │  <<other commands>>         │
                    │  void put(Object e)         │
                    │  void remove()              │
                    └─────────────────────────────┘
```

Figure 11.2 The queue class redesigned for Java

Figure 11.2 shows our modified design.

We will work our way through the methods one by one, adding contracts. We will omit the source code that implements the queue. And we will not repeat the discussion of Chapter 5 that led to the contracts.

11.3.1 THE BASIC QUERY *SIZE()*

The *size()* query does not need a precondition or (like most basic queries) a post-condition. Therefore, it appears in the source listing with just its signature, and a comment giving a brief description of its purpose. By convention, the comment precedes the signature.

```
/**
 * Return the number of elements in the receiver
 */
public int size()
```

11.3.2 THE BASIC QUERY *GET()*

The basic query *get()* is used to inspect the i-th item in the queue (it is common in Java to name queries with verbs, rather than nouns). The query needs a precondition saying that the argument i must be a valid queue position. Because Java has adopted the zero-based counting convention of C++, we will define a queue's items to lie between position *0* and position *size()–1* (of course, we are not saying anything about where a queue's items are actually stored in the implementation). Here is the declaration of *get()*:

```
/**
 * Return the element at position i of the
 * receiver (first element is at position 0).
 *
 * @require i >= 0 && i <= this.size()-1
 */
public Object get(int i)
```

The comment line marked with the *@require* tag is recognized by the iContract preprocessor, which generates additional code in a copy of the source file to test the precondition at runtime and to throw an exception if it is false.

The text following the tag asserts that *i* must lie between 0 and the result of evaluating *size()* –1 on the receiving object, *this*. In Java, **&&** is the logical *and* operator.

11.3.3 THE DERIVED QUERY *HEAD()*

The *head()* query can be specified in terms of the *get()* query because the head of a queue is the item at position zero. The query needs a precondition saying that an empty queue can have no *head()*.

```
/**
 * Return the head element of the receiver
 *
 * @require this.size() >= 1
 *
 * @ensure return == this.get(0)
 */
public Object head()
```

The precondition specifies that the *size()* of the receiving object must be at least 1. The postcondition, introduced by the *@ensure* tag, specifies that the *return* value is equal to the result of performing *get(0)* on the receiver. The == operator is being used in the context of references to objects, so it means "the same object as."

11.3.4 THE DERIVED QUERY *isEmpty()*

The postcondition of the derived query *isEmpty()* ties its *return* value to the *size()* of the receiving object.

```
/**
 * Return true if, and only if, the
 * receiver contains no elements
 *
 * @ensure return == (this.size() == 0)
 */
public boolean isEmpty()
```

Here, the == operator is being used in the context of values of primitive types (specifically, *boolean* and *int* values), so it means "has the same value as."

11.3.5 THE DERIVED QUERY *shallowCopy()*

A shallow copy of a queue has the same *size()* as the queue being copied, and it contains the same elements, in the same order, as the queue being copied.

The first of these assertions translates to the following tagged comment in iContract:

```
 * @ensure return.size() == this.size()
```

Informally, we can specify that two queues contain the same elements, in the same order, by saying

for all valid values of *i*
    the element at position *i* in one of the queues must be
    the same element as the one at position *i* in the other queue.

iContract provides a *forall* operator, which allows us to assert that something is true for a range of integer values. The range of values we are interested in is the valid positions of items in a queue. These range from 0 to *size()–1*. In iContract, the quantified assertion begins as follows:

```
 * @ensure forall int i in 0 .. this.size()-1 |
```

(The vertical bar at the end of the line is a continuation marker.)

For each such position i, we must assert that *get(i)* applied to *this* queue delivers the same object as *get(i)* applied to the queue that *shallowCopy()* returns. Testing for "the same object" involves testing for equal object references, with ==.

The complete contract looks like this:

```
/**
 * Return a shallow copy of the receiver.
 *
 * @ensure return.size() == this.size()
 * @ensure forall int i in 0 .. this.size()-1 |
 *         (this.get(i) == return.get(i))
 */
public Queue shallowCopy()
```

11.3.6 THE CONSTRUCTOR QUEUE

A newly constructed queue must have a *size()* of 0, as specified in the following postcondition on the constructor function *Queue*:

```
/**
 * Construct a new, empty queue
 *
 * @ensure this.size() == 0
 */
public Queue()
```

11.3.7 THE COMMAND *PUT*

Putting an element *e* onto the end of a queue increases the size of the queue and ensures that the item at the end of the queue is the element *e*.

```
/**
 * Add the element e to the end of the receiver
 *
 * @require e != null
 *
 * @ensure this.size() == this.size()@pre + 1
 * @ensure this.get(this.size()-1) == e
 */
public void put(Object e)
```

The precondition specifies a physical constraint that you cannot put null references into a queue.

For the first time, we have a postcondition that needs to refer back to an old value. In iContract, *@pre* is used to signify a value on entry to a method, as in the expression

```
this.size()@pre
```

11.3.8 THE COMMAND *REMOVE*

The Eiffel version of the contract on the *remove* method was this:

remove
-- Remove the oldest item from the queue.
-- Shift the item that used to be in position 2 to
-- the head of the queue.
-- Shift the item that used to be in position 3 to
-- position 2.
-- And so on.
require
not_empty: *count* > 0

ensure

      number_of_items_decreased: *count* = **old** *count* – *1*

      items_shifted: *items.is_equal (***old** *(items.tail)*

The comment explains that removing the oldest item from a queue entails conceptually shifting the item that was in position 2 up to position 1, shifting the item that was in position 3 up to position 2, and so on. We can express this idea neatly with the iContract tool using *forall*. Here is the contract, followed by some explanation.

```
/**
 * Remove the head-element from the receiver
 *
 * @require this.size() >= 1
 *
 * @ensure this.size() == this.size()@pre - 1
 * @ensure forall int i in 0 .. this.size()-2 |
 *     this.shallowCopy()@pre.get(i+1) == |
 *         this.get(i)
 */
public void remove()
```

The precondition says that you cannot remove an item from a queue unless the queue has at least one item in it.

The first part of the postcondition asserts that removing an item from a queue reduces its *size()* by one. The second part of the postcondition occupies three lines.

- The first line quantifies what follows, for all the values of *i* in the range 0 to the final value of *size()* minus 2 (which is, of course, one less than the highest valid position because we are using zero-based counting).
- The second line talks about the object that was at position *(i+1)* in the original queue. By taking a *shallowCopy@pre*, we can talk about the original queue, before the *remove* changed it.
- The third line talks about the object at position *i* in the final queue. Overall, the contract asserts that the object that was at position *(i+1)* in the original queue is the same object as the one now at position *i*, and that this is true for all positions that are now valid.

11.3.9 Summary

That completes our first example of putting contracts into a Java class. These contracts are designed to be preprocessed by a tool called iContract.

The biggest change in moving from the Eiffel version to the Java/iContract version is that we now have a built-in *forall* construct in the assertion language.

We should mention a couple of details about the change from recursive contracts to the version using *forall*:

1. Java supports recursion, so we could have used recursion in Java.
2. Preprocessors that provide *forall* are available for Eiffel and other object-oriented languages.
3. At the time of writing, Eiffel is being extended to provide the power of *forall*.

Java offers designers interfaces *and* classes. We haven't discussed putting contracts on interfaces. That's the main topic of the next section.

11.4 Dictionaries

Chapter 3 presented a contract for a DICTIONARY class. The contract was based on three basic queries: *count*, *has*, and *value_for*. These basic queries were used to specify three commands: *initialize*, *put*, and *remove*.

The source listing showing the contract announced that it was a

class interface
    DICTIONARY [KEY, VALUE]

The *short* form of an Eiffel class, known as a class interface, can be derived automatically from the class by a tool. In Java, by design, interfaces and classes are less tightly coupled. An interface can be implemented by any number of classes, and a class can implement any number of interfaces.

In this section, we see how to place contracts on interfaces so that clients using objects of classes that implement the interfaces do not need to know exactly which classes these objects were created from. (You could carry the ideas we introduce over to languages such as Eiffel, Smalltalk, and C++ that do not provide Java-style interfaces.)

In Java, an interface

1. Lists the methods that can be called on an object of a class that implements the interface. (The iContract tool recognizes tagged comments in interfaces, as well as in classes, so we can add contract information to method declarations in interfaces.)
2. Cannot declare variables. (This is not a problem—in Java, simple queries are declared as functions, not variables.)
3. Cannot declare any constructors. (This is a problem—a contract is not complete without a specification of the properties of a newly created object.)

We overcome the problem in point 3 by introducing a factory class to make dictionary objects and defining an interface for the factory.

The following subsections address:

• Changes to names
• Translating the invariant
• Translating the contracts on all the methods except the constructor
• Introducing a factory interface to constrain the construction of dictionary objects.

11.4.1 NAMES

Here are some changes in terminology we will be making to accommodate Java's conventions:

• **Interfaces.** To make it clear when we are talking about an interface and when we are talking about a class, we will begin the names of interfaces with the letter I, as in *IDictionary.*
• **Dictionaries and Maps.** What we called a dictionary in Chapter 3 is called a map in the Java libraries. We will continue to call it a dictionary. However, the

source code on the Web site includes an implementation of our interface *IDictionary* using the Java library class *Map*.

- **Count and Size.** We will translate Eiffel's *count* property to Java's *size()* property.

- **Keys, Values, and Objects.** In Eiffel, we can make DICTIONARY a generic class and declare that it holds objects of classes KEY and VALUE. In the Java version, we will simply say that a dictionary holds keys of class Object and values of class Object.

- **Underscores and Capitals.** We shall translate each Eiffel *name_with_underscores* to a Java *nameWithCapitals*.

11.4.2 The Invariant

In Eiffel, an invariant comes at the end of a class listing. In iContract, it precedes the declaration of a class or interface (this is consistent with Java's convention of placing comments just before the relevant declarations). Here is the beginning of the listing for the interface *IDictionary*.

```
/**
 * @invariant size() >= 0
 */
public interface IDictionary
```

The invariant asserts that the *size()* of a dictionary is always non-negative.

11.4.3 The Basic Queries

The basic query *size()* needs no contract.

```
/**
 */
public long size();
```

The precondition on *has()*, the test for whether a dictionary has a particular key, precludes a null argument. The postcondition asserts that, if the dictionary is empty, the result of *has()* is false for any key.

```
/**
 * @require key != null
 * @ensure  (size() == 0) implies !return
 */
public boolean has(Object key);
```

The precondition on the look-up function *valueFor()* precludes using a null
argument (a physical constraint) and precludes looking up the value for a key
that is not in the dictionary (a logical constraint).

```
/**
 * @require key != null
 * @require has(key)
 */
public Object valueFor(Object key);
```

11.4.4 A DERIVED QUERY

The postcondition on the derived query *isEmpty()* constrains the *return* value to
be whether the *size()* is 0.

```
/**
 * @ensure  return == (size() == 0)
 */
public boolean isEmpty();
```

11.4.5 THE COMMANDS

The command to *put* a new key and associated value into a dictionary requires
that the key not be null and that the key not be already in the dictionary, and it
ensures that the *size()* increases by 1, that the dictionary now *has()* the key, and
that its associated value is the value just *put()*.

```
/**
 * @require key != null
 * @require !has(key)
 *
 * @ensure size() == size()@pre + 1
 * @ensure has(key)
```

```
 * @ensure valueFor(key) == value
 */
public void put(Object key, Object value);
```

The command to *remove* a key requires that the key not be null and is in the dictionary, and it ensures that the *size()* decreases by 1 and that the dictionary no longer *has()* the key. As a consequence of the dictionary's no longer having the key, there is no *valueFor()* this key, and, for completeness' sake, there is a comment to this effect (a tiny detail—the "//" comment symbols are redundant from the Java compiler's point of view, but they hide the comment from the iContract tool).

```
/**
 * @require key != null
 * @require has(key)
 *
 * @ensure size() == size()@pre - 1
 * @ensure !has(key)
 * //@ensure valueFor(key) undefined
 * //(see precondition on valueFor() )
 */
public void remove(Object key);
```

11.4.6 THE CONSTRUCTOR

The specification of the world of dictionaries is not complete until we have specified the values of the basic queries on a newly created dictionary object. We want to write this specification in an interface. Interfaces cannot contain constructors (because constructors are the business of classes, not interfaces). Therefore, we introduce a factory class with a regular (i.e., nonconstructor) method that returns a newly created dictionary object. Here is the signature of that method:

```
public IDictionary
    newObjectSatisfyingIDictionary();
```

The method returns an object of type IDictionary. Its contract ensures that a newly created dictionary is empty. Here is the complete interface for the factory:

```
public interface IDictionaryFactory {

/**
 * @ensure   return.size() == 0
 */
public IDictionary
   newObjectSatisfyingIDictionary();
}
```

A client wanting to work with a dictionary object will need access to a class that implements this factory interface. Then it can call the *newObjectSatisfyingIDictionary()* method to get a new dictionary object.

11.4.7 A POSSIBLE SET OF CLASSES

We have defined contracts for the IDictionary and IDictionaryFactory interfaces. The UML diagram in Figure 11.3 shows two possible classes that implement these two interfaces.

Class DictionaryUsingMap implements the interface IDictionary (and uses the Java library class Map to do so). Class DictionaryFactory implements the IDictionaryFactory interface.

The dependency between IDictionaryFactory and IDictionary is that the factory must return an object of type IDictionary. Similarly, the dependency between DictionaryFactory and DictionaryUsingMap is that the implementation of the factory must return an object of class DictionaryUsingMap, the class that implements IDictionary (the attached note shows the line of code that achieves this).

11.5   JAVA WITHOUT iCONTRACT

Let us suppose that you want to use some of the ideas of design by contract in your Java programs, but you do not want to use a preprocessing tool such as iContract.

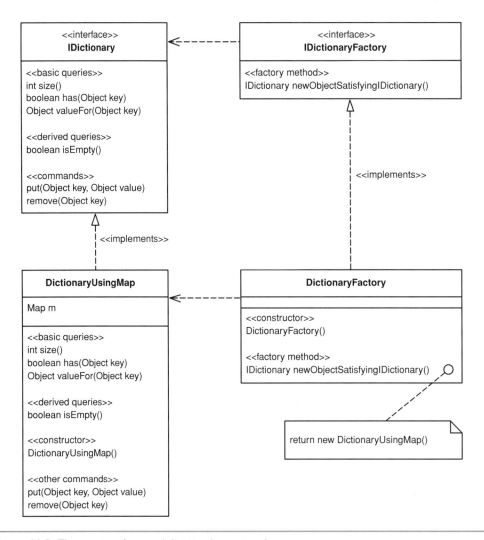

Figure 11.3 The two interfaces and their implementing classes

Preconditions are straightforward—they can be mapped to *if* statements that raise exceptions (an example follows shortly).

Invariants are trickier. You need to write a function to evaluate the invariant, and you need to remember to call that function on entry to, and on exit from, every nonconstructor method, and on exit from every constructor.

Postconditions are the trickiest of all because of the need for old values. You need to remember to write code to store away old values on entry to a method with a postcondition so that you can use these old values to check the postcondition on exit from the method.

We could suggest that you undertake all this extra work in order to have rich contracts. But we think it unlikely you would follow that advice (and it would probably be easier to use a tool such as iContract). Instead, we suggest that you either use a preprocessing tool or just implement preconditions.

In an ideal world, every Java interface would come complete with contracts of the kind discussed in Section 11.4. In the absence of a tool such as iContract, these contracts will just be comments. Of these, the precondition clauses can readily be transformed into code that checks the preconditions.

For example, the contract on the *put* method in interface IDictionary looked like this:

```
/**
 * @require key != null
 * @require !has(key)
 *
 * @ensure size() == size()@pre + 1
 * @ensure has(key)
 * @ensure valueFor(key) == value
 */
public void put(Object key, Object value);
```

The two precondition clauses can each be turned into a statement at the beginning of the implementation of *put* in class Dictionary that raises an exception. Here is the code, followed by some explanation.

```
public void put(Object key, Object value) {
    if (key == null)
        throw new PreconditionException(
            ":DictionaryUsingMap:IDictionary/ put/require key !=
null");
```

```
    if (has(key))
        throw new PreconditionException(
            ":DictionaryUsingMap:IDictionary/put/require
!has(key)");

    m.put(key,value);
}
```

A precondition of the form *require b*, where *b* is a Boolean expression, is turned into an *if* statement of the form:

```
if (!b) throw new PreconditionException( msg );
```

The message has several parts, which describe

- What class of object raised the exception (using the UML convention that *:Name* means an object of class *Name*).
- What interface (if any) the class implements (so that we know where to look for the contract).
- The name of the method that has the failed precondition.
- The precondition that failed. (Because of our experience with Eiffel, we write what the precondition says, rather than what was true when it failed at runtime, which is its opposite. Either convention is fine.)

The normal body of the method comes after the tests for the precondition (in this example, *put* on a dictionary is achieved by calling *put* on the map object *m* that holds the dictionary's keys and values).

The class PreconditionException is defined to extend the Java library class RuntimeException. As a result, the signature of a method that checks a precondition does not have to state that it might throw an exception, and clients do not need to use a *try . . . catch* block when calling the method. This reduces the pollution of the application code caused by the precondition-checking, and it allows the checking code to be removed with hardly any impact (ideally it would be incorporated using conditional compilation so that it can be included or removed automatically).

Our experience has been that the effort of systematically documenting and implementing preconditions is amply rewarded in three ways:

- We think more carefully about our designs, especially about which class is responsible for what.
- The documentation must be up to date, at least as far as preconditions are concerned, or tests fail.
- We occasionally find precondition exceptions being thrown and immediately know where to find the cause of the problem.

11.6   PRECONDITION TESTING

In Chapter 10, we carefully distinguished fulfilling, testing, and checking preconditions.

- A client ought to *fulfill* a precondition.
- A client might or might not *test* a precondition in order to be sure it is fulfilling the precondition.
- A supplier might or might not *check* a precondition in order to be sure that the client did fulfill the precondition.

In our Eiffel examples in Chapters 1 through 10 and in our Java examples so far in this chapter, we have used preconditions as a way of putting a responsibility on clients only to call methods when certain conditions are true. A client that calls a method when a precondition is false is a client with a bug.

In this section, we explore a programming idiom in which a false precondition is not a sign of a bug anywhere in the program. In this idiom, the supplier of a service *checks* a precondition in order to be sure that its clients are well behaved. But it also signals the result of this *check* to the client to save the client from having to *test* the precondition. In effect, the designer collapses an explicit test, such as *isEmpty( )*, and a method that has a precondition based on the test, such as *remove( )*, into a single routine.

We revisit the Queue example from earlier in this chapter to present the idiom, and then discuss it briefly.

Here is the *remove* method in a different version of class *Queue* from the one we explored earlier. The queue is implemented using a vector to store its *elements*.

```
public Object remove() {
    if (elements.size() == 0) {
        throw new QueueEmptyException();
    } else {
        return elements.remove(0);
    }
}
```

When called, this method does three things:

1. It returns the head element of the receiving queue object (so it is a query).
2. It removes the head element of the queue (so it is a command).
3. It throws an exception if it is called when the queue is empty.

The method is a combination of a command and a query. Usually, collapsing a command and a query into one method complicates matters (for example, you then find clients that *remove* an element to inspect it, and have to *put* it back again). However, the collapsing can sometimes be justified in distributed systems on performance grounds. Consider a call by one object to a method in another object. Suppose it takes one unit of time to make the call when both objects are in the same address space. On the same scale, it might take on the order of 100,000 units of time to make the call if the two objects are in different computers connected by a wide area network (WAN). In such an environment, saving calls can be important. One way to save calls is to combine commands and queries.

The method also throws an exception. We now show that this might not signal a bug in the client. The query and the command that have been collapsed into one might look like this, from a contract point of view. There is a *head* query

```
/**
 * Return the head element of the receiver
 *
```

```
 * @require  this.size() >= 1
 *
 * @ensure return == this.get(0)
 */
public Object head()
```

and there is a *remove* command

```
/**
 * Remove the head-element from the receiver
 *
 * @require  this.size() >= 1
 *
 * @ensure this.size() == this.size()@pre - 1
 * @ensure forall int i in 0 .. this.size()-2 |
 *          this.shallowCopy()@pre.get(1+i) == |
 *                              this.get(i)
 */
public void remove()
```

Both these methods have the same precondition, which makes it easier to collapse them into one. The precondition is that the queue is not empty. Here is the collapsed method, with a new name that makes it clearer that it serves two purposes:

```
/**
 * Remove the head element from the receiver,
 * and return it
 *
 * @require  this.size() >= 1
 *
 * @ensure return == this.get(0)@pre
 * @ensure this.size() == this.size()@pre - 1
 * @ensure forall int i in 0 .. this.size()-2 |
 *          this.shallowCopy()@pre.get(1+i) == |
 *                              this.get(i)
 */
public Object removeAndReturnHead()
```

Observe that the postcondition clause defining the return value needs changing to assert that it is the old value of *get()* that is returned.

We can go further. We can remove the precondition and give the method a conditional postcondition, along these lines:

if
    the queue was empty
then
    a signal has been sent saying that it was empty
else
    -- postcondition as before

Here is the method with its precondition removed. Its name has grown, again.

```
/**
 * If the receiver is not empty
 * then remove and return its head element
 * else throw a QueueEmptySignal exception.
 *
 * @require //none
 *
 * @ensure (this.size()@pre == 0) implies |
 *     (this.size() == this.size()@pre)
 * @ensure (this.size()@pre > 0) implies |
 *     (this.size() == this.size()@pre - 1)
 * @ensure (this.size()@pre > 0) implies |
 *     (return == this.get(0)@pre)
 * @ensure (this.size()@pre > 0) implies |
 *     forall int i in 0 .. this.size()-2 |
 *         this.shallowCopy()@pre.get(1+i) == |
 * *                             this.get(i)
 */
public Object
    removeAndReturnHeadOrSignalEmpty() throws
                    QueueEmptySignal {
    if (elements.size() == 0) {
        throw new QueueEmptySignal();
    } else {
        return elements.remove(0);
    }
}
```

A client can now make one call to

- Test if the queue is empty, and, if it isn't
- Get the head element of the queue, and
- Remove the head element from the queue.

Here is a simple piece of client code that empties a queue of Integer objects, printing each element onto the standard output stream.

```
private void emptyQueue( Queue q ) {
    System.out.print(
            "Emptying queue ... elements are:");
    int i;
    boolean moreElements = true;
    while (moreElements) {
        try {
            i = ( (Integer)
                q.removeAndReturnHeadOrSignalEmpty() ).intValue();
            System.out.print( " " + i );
        } catch (QueueEmptySignal qes) {
            moreElements = false;
        }
    }
    System.out.println();
}
```

The loop is controlled by a Boolean variable, *moreElements,* which is set to false when a *QueueEmptySignal* exception is caught. The client *expects* the supplier to raise an exception when the queue is empty and is programmed accordingly. When the supplier raises a *QueueEmptySignal* exception, this does not indicate a bug in the client—it was repeatedly calling *removeAndReturnHeadOrSignalEmpty()* looking for that exception.

We have shown how the *removeAndReturnHeadOrSignalEmpty( )* method can be thought of as performing three tasks: answering the query *head(),* carrying out the command to *remove(),* and answering the query *isEmpty().* (True and false replies are distinguished by raising a *QueueEmptySignal* exception or not.)

This idiom can be useful in distributed systems, to save expensive network calls. It can also be useful in nondistributed, but nevertheless concurrent, programs. A routine such as *removeAndReturnHeadOrSignalEmpty()* can be marked as synchronized, so that only one client program at a time can execute it.

When this idiom is used in practice, it is sometimes presented in disguise:

- The name of the method does not tell you all its tasks.
- The accompanying documentation does not detail all its tasks.
- The accompanying documentation leaves the impression that the exception has something to do with errors, rather than being the chosen way to answer the query *isEmpty()*.

11.7 Things to Do

1. Put an invariant into class Queue.
2. Put back the *capacity* and *isFull* features into class Queue.
3. Introduce a type (represented by an interface) for the type of object to be added to a Queue (called, perhaps, QueueElement).
4. Introduce a type for keys in the Dictionary example. What properties *must* keys have?
5. In the Queue example, introduce two interfaces, one for the nonconstructor methods on a queue, and one for the factory that makes queue objects. Put contracts into these interfaces.
6. In the Java examples, we omitted many header comments in order to highlight the iContract form of assertions. Put them in.
7. Translate other Eiffel examples into Java using a tool such as iContract to provide contracts.
8. Explore using iContract's *forall* to put frame rules into classes Queue and Dictionary.
9. [Harder] The first postcondition clause in the *removeAndReturnHeadOrSignalEmpty()* feature says that if the queue is

empty, it remains empty. In other words, the contract is promising that if the implicit test for *isEmpty()* signals true (by raising an exception), the state of the queue will not change. Why must it make this promise? Explore the consequences of failing to make and keep this promise. Explore how to write the corresponding promise for *put()*. (Hint: You'll need to assert that existing queue items don't change.)

Analysis by Contract

12.1   ABOUT THIS CHAPTER

So far in this book, we have looked at contracts on classes, so we have been working at the program design level. This chapter explores briefly how contracts can be used in analysis models, above the level of program designs. In doing so, it

- Explains one meaning of the term "use case."
- Shows by example how use cases can be specified using a contract. The example is based on a simplified view of bank accounts and cash withdrawals.

12.2   A USE CASE

When you withdraw money from a cash machine at a bank, you use the machine. Withdrawing cash is just one way to use the machine—it is just one use case. Other use cases you might initiate include asking for a balance printed on a slip and changing your PIN. Bank staff have access to another set of use cases, including restocking the ATM with banknotes.

When you initiate a use case, you go through a sequence of interactions with the machine. For the *withdraw cash* use case, the sequence might look like this:

1. You insert your card into the machine.
2. The machine asks for your PIN.
3. You type in your PIN.
4. The machine asks which service you want.
5. You select to withdraw cash.
6. The machine asks how much you want to withdraw.
7. You select an amount to withdraw.
8. The machine dispenses this amount in cash.
9. The machine returns your card.

This is a basic use case description for the *withdraw cash* use case. The full description must also cover alternative paths, such as

- At step 3, the PIN does not match the encrypted copy on the card: The system ejects the card and displays a message, and the use case ends.
- At step 7, the amount you select to withdraw would take your balance below its minimum: The system displays a message that includes the maximum amount you can withdraw and the use case resumes at step 6.

We will not attempt to describe all the details of all the variations. Instead, we will take what we already have and look at it from a different point of view.

Use case descriptions focus on sequences of interactions between a system and the people (and other systems) who use it. These interactions are constrained by business rules, such as "you cannot make a withdrawal that leaves your account balance below its minimum." In the next section, we will model some of these business rules explicitly, and we will omit details of how you interact with the ATM.

12.3   CONTRACTS IN ANALYSIS MODELS

At the level of program designs, we know that a contract for an individual feature abstracts away from the code that implements that feature. We can also use contracts to abstract away from the interaction between a person and an ATM. Let's write a contract for the action of withdrawing cash from an ATM. We'll name the action *withdrawCash* and begin to think about what parameters it has. There's the person withdrawing the cash, the amount they withdraw, and the account they withdraw from. We now have enough information to write the syntax:

withdrawCash(p : Person, a : Account, m : Money)
      -- Person p withdraws amount *m* from account *a*

Just this simple syntax tells us we want to talk about three different types of objects. The UML diagram in Figure 12.1 shows the three types. (Note: In programs, we work with classes of objects. In analysis, we can omit details of how classes are implemented, and concentrate on what properties they have. To remind ourselves that we are working at a level of abstraction above programs, we'll talk about types of objects. If we were to design software for an ATM from our analysis model, we would reintroduce classes to implement these types.)

12.4   A CONTRACT FOR THE *WITHDRAWCASH* USE CASE

An important change that comes about when a person withdraws cash from a cash machine is that the balance of that person's account decreases by the amount withdrawn. We can capture this change in a postcondition.

withdrawCash(p : Person, a : Account, m : Money)
      -- Person *p* withdraws amount *m* from account *a*

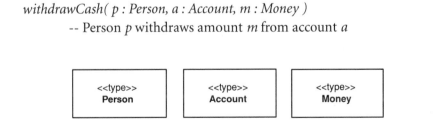

Figure 12.1 Three types to support the signature of *withdrawCash*

ensure
>   account_balance_reduced_by_amount_withdrawn:
>   *a.balance* = **old** *a.balance - m*

This postcondition uses vocabulary that our type model does not capture. Specifically, we want to talk about the balance of an account and about equality and subtraction on money. We need to enrich our type model, as shown in Figure 12.2.

Type *Account* now has a *balance* query of type *Money*. And type *Money* has two queries, one to test equality with some *other* object of type *Money*, and one to return the result of subtracting some *other* object of type *Money*.

If we were to watch a bank in operation, we might see the balance of an account change by some amount withdrawn. But, under some circumstances, the bank might choose not to describe it as someone withdrawing cash. If the person withdrawing the cash were not the account holder, the bank might describe it as a theft, rather than a withdrawal. In other words, there are business rules about such issues as who can withdraw money from an account. By talking to banking experts, we establish that *withdrawCash* has these preconditions:

require
>   withdrawer_holds_account:
>   *p = a.holder*
>   amount_small_enough:
>   *a.balance − m* >= *a.minimum*

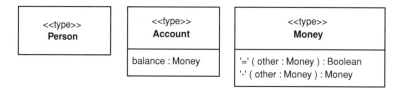

Figure 12.2 An enriched type model

The first condition says you cannot withdraw money unless you are the account holder. The second says that you cannot withdraw so much money that the balance of the account would fall below its minimum (for example, if you were allowed to be $500 overdrawn, your account's minimum would be –$500).

Once again, we need to enrich our type model. We need the model to allow us to talk about the holder of an account, and about the minimum balance of an account, as shown in Figure 12.3.

Now, accounts have a *minimum* balance, modeled as a local query on type *Account*. And accounts have a single *holder*, modeled using an association between type *Account* and type *Person* (the model also allows one person to be the holder of many accounts).

Here are the syntax and contract so far, in one place:

withdrawCash(p : Person, a : Account, m : Money)
        -- Person *p* withdraws amount *m* from account *a*
    require
        withdrawer_holds_account:
            p = a.holder
        amount_small_enough:
            a.balance – m >= a.minimum
    ensure
        account_balance_reduced_by_amount_withdrawn:
            *a.balance = **old** a.balance – m*

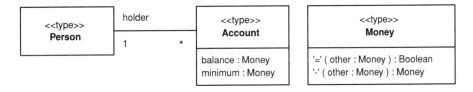

Figure 12.3 A further enriched type model

This contract neatly captures key business rules governing the withdrawing of cash from a bank account. If we were designing a class, rather than capturing business rules, we would call *withdrawCash* a command. And we would make sure that the postcondition specified the effect of *withdrawCash* on the basic queries. Because we are at a level of abstraction well above that of program classes, queries show up in a different way. The type model in Figure 12.3 presents the necessary queries about the world of people, accounts, and money. The type model allows us to talk about such topics as

- The holder of an account
- The accounts of a person
- The balance of an account
- The result of subtracting one sum of money from another

The type model presents the necessary basic queries. We write contracts for units of behavior in terms of these queries (in programming, units of behavior are individual features; in analysis, units of behavior are individual changes in the world being modeled, or individual operations on a system).

12.5 FROM ANALYSIS TO DESIGN

In this section, we offer a simplified view of how an analysis-level contract can be turned into a design. At the heart of the design will be steps that bring about the change specified in the postcondition. But, because the action of withdrawing cash has a precondition, we must take steps to check that the precondition is fulfilled before bringing about this change. And, because the kind of action we have called *withdrawCash* has parameters, we must take steps to identify the actual argument objects in any particular occurrence of a cash withdrawal.

We can outline an interaction between a person wanting to withdraw money and the part of the bank that handles withdrawals. The interaction will concern identifying the argument objects required by the signature, checking that the precondition is fulfilled, and bringing about the changes specified in the postcondition. Here is a possible interaction:

1. Person wanting to withdraw money identifies himself or herself (argument p is now known).

2. Person identifies the account to withdraw from (argument a is now known).

3. System checks that p is the holder of a (one part of precondition has been checked).

4. Person specifies amount to withdraw (argument m is now known).

5. System checks that m will not reduce balance of a below minimum (remainder of precondition has been checked). (All arguments are now known. All assertions in the precondition have been checked.)

6. System dispenses amount m to p and reduces balance of a accordingly (postcondition now true).

This sequence of steps is similar to the sequence presented in Section 12.2. There are two important differences.

First, the sequence is still not a concrete design. It could be implemented by designing a cash machine or by training a cashier. A detailed design for a particular implementation would involve the kind of detail in the sequence in Section 12.2.

Second, it is derived from a contract. In other words, it is a design derived from a specification, rather than being a design that is also being used as a specification.

Partly because the interaction is presented in an abstract form, we can examine it for areas to improve. For instance, steps 2 and 3 could be replaced by steps in which the system presents the accounts that person p holds from which person p picks one. Now the system knows which account to debit and is sure that p is the holder of this account.

12.6   PROBLEM DOMAIN AND SYSTEM MODELS

We have simplified the example, to highlight the way in which contracts can be used in analysis, without getting lost in details. We could enrich the example in several ways. We could explicitly model a number of banks, each with a number of branches. The branches could be connected to allow an account holder to withdraw cash at one branch of one bank from an account held at another branch, perhaps of a different bank. We could explicitly model the cash holding of each branch (which would be reduced when money is withdrawn). We could also model the cash belonging to a person. This would be increased when money is withdrawn. The type model in Figure 12.4 is still a simplification of the world of private bank accounts, but it shows how we might model some of these ideas.

This type model provides a rich set of queries, such as "what is the managing branch of this account?" and "how much cash in hand does this person have?" The action of withdrawing cash at a particular branch might now be specified by this contract:

withdrawCash(p : Person, a : Account, m : Money, b : Branch)
      -- At branch *b*, person *p* withdraws amount of cash *m* from account *a*
require
    withdrawer_holds_account:
      $p = a.holder$
    amount_small_enough:
      $a.balance - m >= a.minimum$
ensure
    person_has_more_cash:
      $p.cashInHand = $ **old** $p.cashInHand + m$
    branch_has_less_cash:
      $b.cash = $**old** $b.cash - m$
    account_balance_reduced:
      $a.balance = $ **old** $a.balance - m$

You could continue the enrichment and capture an invariant that the amount of money in the world does not change because someone withdraws cash from an account. You could extend the type model and the postcondition to model the debt owed by the branch that manages the account to the branch that gave out the cash. You could introduce a new type to model the log that the bank keeps of every withdrawal. And, of course, you could model many other actions, such as opening an account and depositing money into an account.

We will not enrich the models further. Instead, we will briefly highlight the difference between modeling a problem domain and modeling the requirements for a system to be introduced into a domain. We can think of the type model in Figure 12.4, together with the contract for an action, as the beginnings of a model of the key properties of the world of private bank accounts. The model talks about, for instance, objects of type Person, which are the modeling constructs corresponding to real people.

How would the model change if we were trying to specify a system? It would change in several ways. Here are some of them:

- The objects in our type model and in our contracts would now correspond to software objects stored in computers, not to individual people, branches, and so on in the world.
- We should have to pay attention to how to connect things in the world to things in software. For example, a model of the world might talk about individual people. System designers must worry about how to identify people to a system and ask themselves whether it is acceptable to use cards and PINs to identify people, or whether biological properties such as palm prints would be more appropriate.

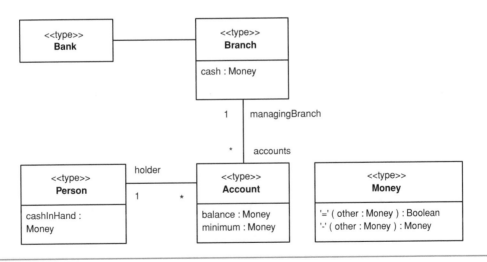

Figure 12.4 Introducing banks and branches

- The system would not keep track of certain aspects of the world of private bank accounts. For example, the computer system at the branch where you hold a bank account does not model the cash you hold. It certainly models how much cash it dispenses, to whom, where, and when, but not your cash holding. So, the type model to support the specification of a required system will omit parts of the problem domain model.

- There would be things to model that were not there before we put a computer system in place, such as a session involving a person and a computer during which we assume the person does not change.

- A system model would need to identify which kinds of people (and other systems) could use the required system. It is easier to build a computer system to support withdrawing cash if the system is to be used only by bank-trained cashiers than if the system is to be used by members of the general public be who are the account holders.

Crucially, however, many of the rules about the business of private bank accounts captured in our model of the problem domain will still apply when we come to specify a required system. The contracts we write to capture business rules, and the type models we devise to support those contracts, are important pieces of domain knowledge that developers must respect when they specify and design systems.

The requirements for a system will come from many sources, including

- Business rules that must be respected (captured in contracts and type models describing a problem domain).

- Choices about what parts of the problem domain to automate (captured in contracts and type models describing an envisioned system).

12.7 THE OBJECT CONSTRAINT LANGUAGE

We have deliberately kept our example simple enough that we can write the assertions in something like a programming language. In practice, analysis level models need a richer language in which to write contracts. The UML modeling language has a sublanguage, called the Object Constraint Language (OCL), in which you can write assertions about UML models. OCL is described in the definition of UML and in a book by two of its designers.

12.8   SUMMARY

In this chapter, we have used a simplified example from the world of private bank accounts to show how behavior can be specified in analysis-level models, using the idea of a *contract* that we introduced in the context of program design. We sometimes use the phrase "analysis by contract" to describe what we are doing.

Our notion of basic queries has changed a little. Basic queries are now introduced by drawing a model of the types of objects relevant to our discussions. Commands assert changes to the properties of such type models.

However, the change in our notion of basic queries is not really a big change. If we think back to the world of classes and program designs, we have encountered queries that can be shown on class diagrams. For example, in the observer pattern in Chapter 9, we talked about the set of observers attached to a subject and drew a class diagram showing the relevant association.

Taken together, a type model and the contracts on commands can capture our understanding of how part of the world works and can form part of the requirements for any system to be introduced into that world. A type model and contracts can also capture choices about what aspects of a world are to be automated.

The theme throughout this book has been this:

- You want to specify the pieces of behavior exhibited by an abstraction (until this chapter, that meant a set of features on a class, but now it includes whole systems and even aspects of the world these systems inhabit).
- You build a conceptual model of the abstraction to give yourself a suitable set of queries about the abstraction.

- You list the commands that can affect these queries—the commands can be features on a class, or operations on a system, or ways in which people and machines change the world around them.
- You specify the effects of the commands on the conceptual model (i.e., the queries).

Bibliography

This short bibliography lists sources of information on the tools and techniques used in this book (Design by Contract, UML, Eiffel, Java, the Observer pattern, and iContract). It also suggests two starting points for searching for information on related topics.

DESIGN BY CONTRACT

Design by contract is described by its creator in the following book, along with many principles and practices of object-oriented design and programming (the book has an extensive bibliography):

- Meyer, B. *Object-oriented software construction*, 2nd ed. Prentice Hall, 1997.

The principles of how to develop good contracts were first published in

- McKim, J. C., Jr. *Class interface design and programming by contract.* Mingins, C., Duke, R., Meyer, B. (eds.), *Proceedings of TOOLS 18 (TOOLS Pacific)*, Prentice Hall, November 1995, 433–470.

Chapter 6 mentions alternative redefinition rules for subclasses that reuse code but do not claim to be subtypes. These can be found in

- Mitchell, R., Howse, J., and Maung, I. *As-a: A relationship to support code reuse. Journal of Object-Oriented Programming*, Vol. 8, No. 4, 1995, p. 25–33, 55.

Chapter 8 discusses design by contract and defensive programming, a theme explored in

- McKim, J., and Henderson-Sellers, B. *Programming by contract: What's in it for the supplier?* In Ege, R., Singh, M., Meyer, B. (eds.), *Proceedings of TOOLS 14*, Prentice Hall, August 1994.

Chapter 9 mentions contracts for the immutable set class. They are developed in

- Mitchell, R., Howse, J., and Hamie, A. *Contract-oriented specifications.* In *Proceedings of TOOLS 24*, Chen, J., Li, M., Mingins, C., and Meyer, B. (eds.), IEEE, 1997.

THE UNIFIED MODELING LANGUAGE, UML

The graphical design notation used in the examples is the Unified Modeling Language (UML). The definitive source of information about UML is the Object Management Group (OMG). Their Web site is at

- www.omg.org

Here's a short and highly readable introduction to UML:

- Fowler, M. *UML Distilled. Applying the standard object modeling language*, 2nd Ed., Addison-Wesley, 1999.

UML's object constraint language, OCL, is described in

- Warmer, J., and Kleppe, A. *The object constraint language. Precise modeling with UML.* Addison-Wesley, 1999.

THE EIFFEL AND JAVA PROGRAMMING LANGUAGES

The Eiffel programming language is described in

- Meyer, B. *Eiffel: The language.* Prentice Hall, 1992.

The Java programming language is described in

- Arnold, K., Gosling, J., and Holmes, D. *The Java programming language.* Addison-Wesley, 2000.

THE OBSERVER PATTERN

The Observer pattern discussed in Chapters 9 and 10, and many other interesting patterns, are described in

- Gamma, E., Helm, R., Johnson, R., and Vlissides, J. *Design patterns.* Addison-Wesley, 1995.

The Observer pattern is also discussed in

- Jézéquel, J .M., Train, M., and Mingins, C. *Design patterns and contracts.* Addison-Wesley, 1999.

COMPILERS AND PREPROCESSORS

Compilers for Eiffel (which incorporates design by contract) are available from several organizations, including:

- http://www.eiffel.com/ (Interactive Software Engineering, the home of Eiffel)
- http://www.halstenbach.com/ (Halstenbach ACT GmbH)
- http://www.object-tools.com/ (Object Tools GmbH)
- http://smalleiffel.loria.fr/ (SmallEiffel (GNU Eiffel) from LORIA)

The iContract preprocessor for Java is available from:

- www.reliable-systems.com

THREE USEFUL WEB SITES

This book has an associated Web site at:

- http://cseng.aw.com/book/0,3828,0201634600,00.html

The following Web site points to thousands of other sites related to object technology. The site is organized around indexes, so it's usually easy to find information.

- http://www.cetus-links.org

The NEC Research Institute provides a search facility for papers on computing topics at the following Web site (you can use it to do citation (i.e., forward) searches to see who has referenced a particular paper or book—an extremely useful facility):

- http://citeseer.nj.nec.com/cs

Index